Successful Digital Transformation Initiatives
in SMEs

Anna Marrucci • Riccardo Rialti

Successful Digital Transformation Initiatives in SMEs

A Relational Goods Perspective

Anna Marrucci
University of Pisa
Pisa, Italy

Riccardo Rialti
University of Milan
Milan, Italy

ISBN 978-3-031-36464-8   ISBN 978-3-031-36465-5   (eBook)
https://doi.org/10.1007/978-3-031-36465-5

Cover illustration: Pattern © Melisa Hasan

This Palgrave Macmillan imprint is published by the registered company Springer Nature Switzerland AG.
The registered company address is: Gewerbestrasse 11, 6330 Cham, Switzerland

PREFACE

SMEs make up more than the 95% of businesses operating worldwide, and these firms are fundamental assets in any national economy. Many innovations often originate in SMEs, and a large percentage of the world's population works either in a micro, small, or medium enterprise. These firms make up the fabric of the economic system and are often key suppliers for their larger counterparts. SMEs are often late-comers, lagging behind when it comes to digitalization projects (Frederico, 2021). This can often lead to problems related to competitivity through loss of control or lower margins. Scholarly literature has paid little attention to the possible solutions that could be used to address this problem. Moreover, extant research has mostly focused on the role of technological characteristics and economic incentives, pushing SMEs toward digital transformation. As with any business transformation, the selected change management strategy is fundamental in driving transformation. Building on this, this book brings the analysis back to SMEs' roots, focusing on employees. Using a relational goods-based perspective, the authors seek to understand how relationships existing between groups of employees and between staff and managers are fundamental in facilitating successful digital transformation in SMEs.

Pisa, Italy
Milano, Italy

Anna Marrucci
Riccardo Rialti

Contents

ABOUT THE AUTHORS

Anna Marrucci is a PhD Candidate in Management and Business Administration at the University of Pisa (IT) and a Didactic Assistant at the University of Florence (IT). She is also Adjunct Professor of Management at IED—Istituto Europeo di Design. Her principal research interest concerns the role of humanistic management in I4.0 endeavors. She has published several book chapters for international publishers, such as Taylor and Francis, Emerald, and Palgrave. Her research has also been published in international journals, such as *MD*, *CIT*, and *BFJ*. Over the last two years, she has attended several international conferences, including European Academy of Management (EURAM), Academy of Management Conference (AoM), and Global Fashion Marketing Conference (GFMC). Her doctoral dissertation concerns the analysis of the mechanisms used to improve the digitalization of SMEs in the industrial sector.

Riccardo Rialti is Assistant Professor of Management at the Department of Economics, Management, and Quantitative Methods at the University of Milan (IT). Previously, he has been a Research Fellow and Adjunct Professor of Management, and he achieved his PhD in Business Administration and Management at the University of Pisa (IT) in 2019. He has been a visiting faculty member at University of Lincoln (UK), Middlesex University London (UK), Sophia University (JAP), and ESCP Europe (FR). His main research interests are related to digital technologies in management and marketing. Over the years, his research has primarily focused on big data, organizational dynamic capabilities, knowl-edge management, and ambidexterity. His papers have been published in international journals such as *JBR*, *IEEE-TEM*, *TFSC*, *MD*, *BPMJ*, *CIT*, *BFJ*, *JGM*, and *WREMSD*. In recent times, Riccardo has been working as a strategic consultant for SMEs wishing to digitalize to expand their business.

LIST OF FIGURES

CHAPTER 1

Introduction

Abstract The purpose of the book is to explore the importance of humanistic management postulated in fostering digital transformation in small and medium enterprises (SMEs). Relational goods have been identified as the main theoretical lens under which explore how humanistic principles could diffuse in the business and thereby change human attitude and behavior in respect of digital technologies underlying digital transformation. To do so, first literature on relational goods have been reviewed. Likewise, the authors examined literature on digital transformation and about Diffusion of Innovation Theory. Finally, a real-world case has been explored to assess the importance of such a kind of intangible goods on digital transformation.

Keywords Humanistic management • Human behavior • Relational goods • Business ethics • Digital technologies • Digital transformation

Over the last decade, researchers have paid increased attention to the importance of adapting humanistic principles to business strategies. Humanism is an ensemble of philosophical approaches which guide human behavior in respect of others, advocating for the need to respect each other as individuals in order to allow for self-realization (Martin & Freeman, 2004). This approach values the individual, respects their autonomy and freedom to choose how to live their life, and emphasizes the importance of human relationships, recognizing the interconnectedness and mutual dependency of people. It encourages building strong relationships based on respect, understanding, and compassion, with the goal of creating a society in which people can work together to build a better future (Carr et al., 2017). Humanistic principles advocate for education to be accessible to all and for knowledge to be used to create a better world. Additionally, these principles support justice and equality, recognizing that all people are of equal worth and should be treated with respect and dignity (Pirson, 2017).

The application of humanistic values in management has shown how companies can become better work environments, in which individuals value their participation in the business community more than their personal fulfillment. Employees are empowered, willing to collaborate, and honest in respect of others. The ethical principles of identity and self-recognition are fundamental and need to span the entire organization in order to create engagement. Employees tend to value each other's contribution in a fair way and to report the contribution of everyone to upper echelons (Pirson, 2017).

However, what is missing in current literature is the consideration of the importance of humanistic principles in digital transformation projects, particularly in small and medium enterprises (SMEs). These businesses need to digitally transform in order to keep up with their larger competitors, but often lack the resources, time, or competencies to do so (Hirman et al., 2019). In such a regard, they may try to overcome some of these barriers by nurturing the engagement their employees have with the company, in order to convince the workforce of the urgency of the transformation and the need to learn new skills. This is where humanistic principles come into play.

Very often, SMEs already follow these principles implicitly, as managers tend to know everyone involved in the business and their personal background. Additionally, many SMEs in diverse contexts have started to invest in training programs in order to create better business environments, due to their difficulty in hiring new employees (Dierksmeier, 2020).

Following these perspectives, the purpose of this book is to explore the role played by one of the pivotal elements of the humanistic perspective, that is, relational goods, and the impact they have on the success of digital transformation. Relational goods are a particular kind of intangible goods which may exist within businesses when employees start to develop intersubjective relationships with peers and recognize each other's skills and talents. They are goods arising from the relationship between different individuals, making people think in terms of "us" instead of "I," and creating a workplace in which everyone is aiming for the same objectives.

The authors focused on several Italian SMEs operating in the same industry and belonging to the same owners and carried out a qualitative and quantitative analysis to reinforce the robustness of their findings. The book is structured as follows: the first chapter deals with the definition of relational goods through the observation of philosophical approaches; the second chapter contextualizes the meaning of digital transformation and the importance of humanistic management principles in transformation management; the third one explains the positioning of the relational goods construct within the Diffusion of Innovation Theory (DOI); the fourth presents the analysis; the fifth provides guidelines for managers.

It will start with a section explaining the growing attention toward a new humanism in business management. Definitions of humanism and humanistic management will also be outlined to describe the broader phenomenon. In this vein, we will also provide an excursus on the importance of using humanistic approaches in the management of human resources, which represent the main value of the business. People will thereby be considered as the most relevant *resource* of any business, a view also shared by practice-based view.

Humans are also the one making machines working, and it is necessary to unpack their role in technology adoption using theory not only based on technology usefulness (Rapp, 1985).

After these points, we will explore the importance of the research in the current environment.

REFERENCES

Carr, S. C., Parker, J., Arrowsmith, J., Haar, J., & Jones, H. (2017). Humanistic management and living wages: A case of compelling connections? *Humanistic Management Journal, 1*, 215–236.

Dierksmeier, C. (2020). From Jensen to Jensen: Mechanistic management education or humanistic management learning? *Journal of Business Ethics, 166*(1), 73–87.

Hirman, M., Benesova, A., Steiner, F., & Tupa, J. (2019). Project management during the Industry 4.0 implementation with risk factor analysis. *Procedia Manufacturing, 38*, 1181–1188.

Martin, K. E., & Freeman, R. E. (2004). The separation of technology and ethics in business ethics. *Journal of Business Ethics, 53*, 353–364.

Pirson, M. (2017). *Humanistic management: Protecting dignity and promoting well-being.* Cambridge University Press.

Rapp, F. (1985). Humanism and technology: The two-cultures debate. *Technology in Society, 7*(4), 423–435.

CHAPTER 2

Human Relations Importance in Modern Business: An Ontological Perspective

Abstract Relational goods are intangible goods which may arouse as a consequence of relationships existing between two or more individuals. They originate from intersubjectivity and reflexivity in human relations. In the case of their emergence, the relationship is capable to generate sense, and the involved individuals will start to nurture their belonging to the partnership. While relational goods have been scantly explored, their origins trace their roots in classical and modern philosophy. As the majority of individuals spend the most of their daily life in the workplace, how these goods may emerge even in such context will be explored.

Keywords Relational goods • Human relations • Sense-making • Intersubjectivity • Reflexivity • Business ethics • Humanism

2.1 Philosophical Foundations of Human Relationships

Theoretical developments in relational economics suggest that the success of sustainable economic growth depends on the quality of interpersonal relationships (Zamagni, 2006, 2008). This perspective implies that any instance of economic flourishing can occur only when accompanied and supported by individuals' growth, as well as their subjectivity and the mutual recognition they experience. In other words, it has become

A. Marrucci, R. Rialti, *Successful Digital Transformation Initiatives in SMEs*, https://doi.org/10.1007/978-3-031-36465-5_2

evident that relationships with others, and the quality of these relationships, are necessary for both identity formation and psychological wellbeing. Moreover, relationships need to be considered key elements triggering social transformation, promoting social change (Zinkin & Brown, 1996), and affecting economic development (Barone, 2006). To grasp the meaning of a social relationship, we need to understand its roots and analyze its two main elements: identity and recognition. These two aspects recall ethical and philosophical origins, as they can be considered fundamental factors influencing human behavior. Therefore, by following this perspective, we are able to operationalize the meaning of the relationship and understand what levers need to be managed in order to promote new social developments or changes. Identity and recognition are two primary needs that condition the individual and the quality of his or her social relationships. If social relations need to go beyond their mere instrumental definition, they should fulfill the individual's unique requirements through recognition processes. In sum, a "social relationship" exists when individuals act as custodians of freedom and their personal nature is recognized. Respect for identity leads to the creation of social relationships based on mutual trust and full acceptance, transcending the view of an instrument only capable of achieving a specific purpose. In societies lacking a shared set of values and meanings, individuals may struggle to orientate themselves, leading to a crisis of meaning. This can be the result of population growth, industrialization, and media proliferation, all of which can lead to multiple different ways of thinking and living. Such dynamism can be a source of disorientation, as individuals must constantly search for a sense of self amidst a multitude of choices. It is no longer possible to assume a single universally accepted value system, which means that personal and social identity can no longer coincide. As a result, individuals not recognizing themselves and their identity may be threatened or even destroyed. The development of personal identity can lead to greater autonomy, allowing an individual to be less dependent on the approval of others and more resilient to manipulation. Embracing one's own uniqueness also regard giving respect to the autonomy of others, as their differences should be accepted and not reduced to any social roles (Crespi, 2004). Aristotle, in *The Politics*, argued that humans are social animals, meaning they are inclined to form societies and cooperate with one another. This concept encompasses both the idea of sociality and their capacity to benefit from living in a group (Zamagni, 2006). Economics has largely focused on the concept of advantages obtained from relationships, neglecting the importance of interpersonal relationships, reciprocity, and ethical values. This has led to the conception of the *homo oeconomicus*—a being whose decisions are solely driven by rational principles and the maximization of personal utility. However, it is now widely accepted that this does not fully explain the behavior of economic agents. Scholars have thus suggested that the *homo oeconomicus* should also be seen as a being whose choices are motivated by intrinsic factors, such as ethics, identity, and love (Borzaga & Depedri, 2005). This allows for a more comprehensive understanding of human behavior. Accordingly, the concept of rational choice should be extended to include the idea that satisfaction is derived from a sense of identity (Bénabou & Tirole, 2006). Finally, Zamagni (2006) argued that the limits of rational choice can be seen in the fact that people are intrinsically relational and make decisions not only for themselves but also with and between others. According to a philosophical approach, human beings exist in a context of social relations, without which they would not be able to exist and thrive (Maritain, 1947). Maritain emphasizes how vital these relationships are, noting that individuals cannot subordinate themselves to society, as the common good is inextricably linked to the good of persons in society. Moreover, he posits that humans are endowed with both physical and psychological freedom, which allows them to be the masters of their own destiny. This moral freedom, or freedom of independence, is the ability to freely be oneself. Donati (2019) further explains that when two or more individuals interact and care for a relationship by respecting each other, relational goods can emerge. These relational goods arise from relationships with structures that acknowledge the intangible and crucial aspects of human life: uniting the terms of the relationship while still respecting differences.

These statements will be further analyzed in the following paragraphs.

2.1.1   *Plato and Aristotle's Philosophical Views on Relationships*

In order to comprehend the authentic essence of a social relationship, beyond its mere instrumental categorization, it is necessary to examine how some ancient philosophers have approached this topic. Indeed, ancient philosophy can offer valuable contributions in enabling us to understand the structural elements that form a connection between individuals. This paragraph seeks to explore how two of the most influential philosophers of ancient Greece, Plato and Aristotle, have conceptualized identity and relationships, in order to illustrate the foundations of social relations.

To gain an understanding of Plato's perspective on identity and relationship, it is paramount to investigate the connection between the actual and relativism, which the philosopher illustrates using the metaphor of the cave. In the parable, captives are chained to a wall on which the images of humans and other objects are projected. The prisoners assume that the shadows are the only genuine reality. When one of them is set free, he recognizes that what he had believed to be real was merely the projection of something more authentic than the shadows he had observed. According to this, human beings inhabit a visible world that is limited, and what lies beyond is the journey to the world of Ideas. From a Platonic standpoint, the Theory of Forms postulates that the visible reality is merely an imitation of a perfect, immutable realm. This realm, which is the basis of the universe, is an ideal, unseen reality. Thus, the visible world in which people reside would, in this case, be an imitation of the perfect and unchanging universe. The main purpose of Platonism is to make nature an illusion and to judge it in relation to a moral Idea that surpasses it (Smith, 2005, p. 99). In this way, the difference between rivals is to determine which one is a faithful copy of the Idea or of the perfect and immutable realm. This disparity from the Idea allows us to reach a new concept: that difference is what defines reality. In fact, since the imitations that compose our context are a combination of reality and deviations from the ideal, these same differences create and promote new insights. Thus, inner uniqueness is the true identity of things and people, beyond any surface resemblance. This perspective shows us how the reality of things can only be recognized if related to an ideal Form. Respect and recognition of diverse identities can foster different perspectives and ideas. Moreover, the arena in which similarities and differences are appreciated and highlighted are relationships in that differences emerge only when related to something and someone else.

Aristotle had a distinctive view on the matter of identity and relations, which differed from that of Plato. He declared that the perception of an idea is actually the idea itself (Rossitto, 1993). According to the philosopher, identity is an intrinsic characteristic of a being, not an outcome of its alliance with an idea. To back up this belief, Aristotle based his approach on three fundamental concepts: substance, accident, and category. He depicted substance as the essential core of a thing; that is, what leads a thing to be what it is and nothing else. The notion of accident, exemplified in the *Metaphysics*, is something that is a fact pertaining to a thing but is not necessarily pertinent to it. Accidents are those varying qualities of different elements. Aristotle also researched the idea of category, which he regarded as the most elevated form of homogeneous predicates or entities (Bonelli & Masi, 2011). His ultimate conclusion was that essence, as the ultimate form of substance, serves as the basis of relation in humans. Indeed, because essence distinguishes one thing from another, essence itself encourages and respects diversity, which is a core concept of human relationships. This relational sense is the collective and interdependent character of individual items, bound by different essences.

These two authors argued that, in a world of imitations, purer identities represent new realities. The differences that exist between the imitation and the Ideal realm create a new truth. These statements enhance the concept of difference, which can only emerge in relation to something else. Identity allows us to be different from one another, and this diversity creates new knowledge. As Aristotle argued, the essence of things and individuals is the truthful part because it is what a thing is, which shows us how it differs from all other things. These differences make individuals unique and can only be valued in relation to each other.

2.1.2 Hegelian and Christian Perspectives About Relationships

In re-examining the theories of Plato and Aristotle, we have determined how respect for differences can foster the creation of individual identities in the realm of social relations. Moreover, Aristotle stressed that the need to conceive relationships is an essential part of the human experience. Connections, then, join, produce, and create. To fully comprehend the many meanings associated with relationships, a multidisciplinary approach is required. In fact, to further investigate the concept of relationships, it is essential that we introduce the notion of a triadic relationship. In the Encyclopedia (1830/2017), Hegel defines the dialectical moment as the elimination of finite determinations and their passage into contrary determinations. As such, these determinations must accept the veracity of their opposition in order to be themselves: "the opposite reveals itself as the condition of their existence" (Cortella, 1996, p.2). Dialectics is both the progression of determinations toward negation and the opening of determinations toward the truth: "in the opposite, determination finds not only the criticism of itself but also its profound truth" (Cortella, 1996, p.3). Dialectics are shown to have positive outcomes, as they correspond to the truth in which thesis and antithesis are transformed into synthesis. The

Hegelian formula strives to understand everything using an immanent and self-generating logic that eliminates transcendence (Donati, 2016). Despite this, there is an alternative dialectic that differs from the Hegelian concept—the Christian Trinity. The generative nature of the Christian Trinitarian relationship has been translated into a metaphysics of negativity, interpreted as a vital category. In the New Testament, God is identified as three distinct Persons united within their relationships. In particular, the Trinitarian relationship is derived from the belief in the Son, whose being is an exclusively ontological relationship with the Father (Donati, 2016). Father, Son, and Spirit represent eternal and uncreated natures, with all other existing natures considered to be ontologically dependent on this first nature. Each reality only exists within its relationship with others. In this way, the foundation of the human being rediscovers a dimension of freedom that is deeply rooted in the immanence of the triune God. On an ontological level, the Father, the Son, and the Spirit, although distinct, are one, with one identical substance. Even in these notions, the concept of difference and opposites emerges again. With and through others, we can understand the specificities of individuals and realize that despite our differences, we all tend toward oneness. The relationship pursues the purpose of valuing the different with the purpose of unifying.

2.1.3   *The Generative Perspective of Human Relationships*

Previous scholars have suggested that social relationships should promote the distinctiveness of the individuals involved. It is essential that we recognize the autonomy and uniqueness of each relationship, while simultaneously engaging in a process of synthesis in order to reach a unified and generative outcome. Identity, differences, and generativity are thus fundamental components of a non-instrumental social relationship. The constructive processes outlined by Edgar Morin (1977–2004) in *La Methode* reflects the idea that reality is a result of the activity of society structures. His theory of complexity does not oppose order and disorder but instead attempts to unite them in a dialogic circle. This circle is symbolic of the relationships between the individual, society, and species, in which individuals are imprinted with culture. Human beings have the capacity to exhibit rationality, delirium, hybris, and destructiveness, which can be used as a source of creation. The awareness of being part of various relationships and social systems can help us to embrace self-reflexive consciousness, and these aspects lead to the conceptualization of multiplex unites, in which diversity is integral to the unity of life. Disorder and chaos are not only unavoidable obstacles but may also present possibilities for creation. Consequently, each relationship becomes an opportunity for change, and by perceiving and desiring an event, something is made possible and tangible. In this way, when synthesized through reflective processes, individual differences can create social relationships.

The preceding paragraphs have provided a summary of the views of some philosophers with regard to social relationships. In particular, the analysis has centered around three essential aspects: individual identity, differences, and generative conception. These different strands of thought suggest that in order to facilitate a concrete understanding of social relationships, it is necessary for us to first consider the personal identities of the participants, recognize the differences and particularities of individuals, and strive for synthesis or generative reflection. In short, a relationship can only promote personal and social growth if it allows individuals to reflect on and accept the diversity of others. The fullest manifestation of identity and difference can only occur in a relationship, that is, in an intersubjective exchange. Synthesis and generative attainment can only arise through reflexivity, which the relationship should promote. Through the relationship, one individual can consider what the other desires and thinks, eventually leading to an understanding and acceptance of the other. Intersubjectivity and reflexivity are thus the highest forms of a social relationship, as they contain the prerequisites of identity, difference, and generativity.

2.2   Emerging Importance of Relational Goods

A philosophical approach grants us the opportunity to emphasize how identity, differences, and the generation of meaning are integral components of all relationships. These features can be summarized in two larger constructs: intersubjectivity and reflexivity. Every relationship necessitates the exchange and encounter between two or more individuals, each of whom brings their own identity and distinctions. The notions of intersubjectivity and reflexivity have been explored in the works of the sociologist Pierpaolo Donati, who explained how each social relationship is structured by these two components. Donati (2019) has proposed a novel view of the relationship between individuals, wherein it is seen to emerge from interactions, yet possess a reality of its own, even in the absence of communication and exchange. Central to this notion are the concepts of intersubjectivity and reflexivity, both of which are intrinsic aspects of the relationship. Notably, reflexivity is of particular ethical importance, as it necessitates taking responsibility for one's own actions, both toward oneself and toward one's partner. This notion of intersubjectivity has been widely employed within the field of psychology (Doherty, 2008), and social sciences more generally (Mori & Hayashi, 2006), encompassing ideas related to shared understanding and mutual awareness. Coelho Jr and Figueiredo (2003) conceptualize intersubjectivity as an implicit behavioral orientation, while Donati and Solci (2011) propose the integration of intersubjectivity and reflexivity when analyzing the emergent phenomenon of their mutual influence. The emergent effect has been recognized as a quality that arises from a relationship. For this to occur, it is essential to promote interactions that are accompanied by more reflective and sophisticated forms of intersubjectivity. Therefore, it is important to consider and understand reflexive aspects when examining the relevancy of relationships. Sandywell (2013) has conceptualized reflexivity as an act of questioning interpretive systems. Moreover, Greene (1995) has proposed that reflexivity allows us to move beyond experience-based understandings of organizational structure when confronting a social world contaminated by something imperceptible. The aim of reflexivity is to unearth and understand those imperceptible assumptions and conceive new possibilities. As such, reflexivity works to bring human creativity to the forefront of technical, political, and institutional processes (Sandywell, 2013). It has been argued that personal development only takes place when one individual acknowledges the other (2013, p. 134). The combination of intersubjectivity and reflexivity assists in the formation of a social relationship that is beneficial for both parties through mutual education. In addition, intersubjectivity and reflexivity have the potential to generate new realizations, which serve as the foundation for an individual's advancement and development.

In accordance with Donati's perspective, when relationships are based on intersubjectivity and reflexivity, they can potentially foster both personal and social growth. These relationships can be categorized as relational goods, which are beneficial beyond the instrumental realm and provide an opportunity for communicative processes, the development of meaning, and transformation. Donati (2014) further highlight the importance of not reducing relational goods to the benefits they bring to individuals, as this would misrepresent their value. Rather, interest in relational goods should be based on the aim of achieving a shared good, rather than pursuing private benefits.

2.2.1 The Re-discovery of Relational Thinking to Cope with Current Crises

Historically, economic analysis has neglected to consider the significance of interpersonal relationships. In particular, theories interpreting interactions between workers and employers have often conceptualized the relationship as a market exchange (Borzaga & Depedri, 2005). Despite the growing recognition that relationship climate can shape employee attitudes and, consequently, a company's performance, interpersonal and reflexive relationships have rarely been studied. Empirical research has primarily focused on relational goods in the context of nonprofit organizations and social cooperatives, as the goals of these entities are congruent with the characteristics of these types of relationships. Borzaga and Depedri (2005) conducted a study to assess the value that employees in the social services sector placed on interpersonal aspects. Their results demonstrated that interpersonal relationships had a strong influence on employee satisfaction, irrespective of salary level. Donati and Solci (2015) further explored the importance of relational goods in for-profit businesses by analyzing their correlation with business performance indicators, such as competitiveness, job creation, and profitability. Their results indicate that companies that generate low levels of relational goods experience poorer profitability, higher staff turnover, and reduced customer loyalty. Consequently, management scholars should be aware of the role of relational goods and their capacity to give businesses a competitive edge. In order to effectively manage businesses in the post-COVID-19 world, it is essential that we foster the creation of a culture based on reciprocal relationships. This demonstrates management's dedication to the needs and expectations of their employees, while simultaneously inspiring intrinsic motivation, social progress, coherence, and innovation (Grootaert & van Bastelaer, 2002; Guiso et al., 2004; Routledge & von Amsberg, 2003). The generation of this culture is critical in overcoming the current economic, institutional, and relational crisis affecting all sectors of contemporary society. It is also necessary for us to address the individualistic isolation caused by the pandemic, as well as generate solutions that consider the intricate dynamics of socioeconomic systems (Donthu & Gustafsson, 2020). Traditional economic models have proven to be inadequate when it comes to facilitating a better understanding of how organizations can handle emerging uncertainties. Similarly, dated business models are unable to guarantee the production of a competitive benefit through contemporary practices (Brammer et al., 2020). In this context, it appears that capitalism is unsustainable in the long run, as profits must be supplanted by concerns for the safety and welfare of individuals (McClure et al., 2020). As a result, organizations need to consider new strategies to maintain morale and employee satisfaction (McClure et al., 2020). In this regard, research has been devoted to exploring how organizations can nurture employee well-being and thus allow firms to continue to function profitably. Two primary solutions have been identified as effective in augmenting job performance. On the one hand, providing monetary or nonmonetary incentives may be a suitable solution when it comes to motivating employees. In fact, salary increases, along with several other benefits, have been seen to stimulate workforces and enhance work performance. On the other hand, solutions geared toward improving working conditions and transforming workplace relationships have been deemed suitable for creating a positive work environment. Among these components that create better atmospheres, relational goods may play a primary role (Donati, 2014, 2019) because relationships represent the foundation of human well-being (Marrucci et al., 2020, 2022).

2.3   What Are Relational Goods?

The notion of "relational goods" was initially suggested by four academics: Martha Nussbaum (philosopher, 1986), Benedetto Gui (economist, 1987), Carole Uhlaner (political scientist, 1989), and Pierpaolo Donati (sociologist, 1986). Nonetheless, more recently, Becchetti et al. (2008) provided a holistic definition that summarizes the primary elements of this concept, expressed as "the affective/expressive and non-instrumental part of human relationships" (Becchetti et al., 2008, p. 343). Scholars have widely recognized Martha Nussbaum's work, *The Fragility of Goodness* (1986), as a seminal contribution when exploring the genesis of the notion, where goods are understood in a purely moral sense and are expressed as friendship, love, and political commitment. According to Nussbaum (1996), the production of relational goods is limited to a select group of individuals who share a common experience (Solci, 2009). Additionally, both physical and emotional distance can hinder the creation of these goods. Although Nussbaum's view provides a philosophical understanding of the concept of relational goods, it does not offer a generalizable theory (Donati, 2019). In contrast, Gui (1987) provides a different interpretation of relational goods, characterizing them as "goods that are not material and that do not depend on the services that are consumed individually, but are linked to interpersonal relationships" (p. 37). Unlike Nussbaum, Gui states that these goods are products of the relationship, and their presence is contingent upon certain outputs. The concept of relational goods, which the researcher has termed an "encounter" (Gui, 2005), is based on the premise that there is face-to-face interaction between two or more parties. This could involve, for instance, a transaction between a real estate agent and a customer, or a manager providing job instructions to a new employee. In addition to the tangible outputs of these encounters, intangible benefits can also be derived, referred to as relational goods. To illustrate his point, the author uses the example of a barber-customer relationship, where the establishment of a friendly relationship between the barber and the customer generates extra value that is classified as a relational good. The objective, then, is to demonstrate that even in the context of economic transactions, human beings can obtain a sense of moral and emotional satisfaction. From a sociological perspective, Solci (2009) has noted that reducing relational goods to their affective component is overly simplistic. In fact, Uhlaner (1989) defines relational goods as something that can be possessed only through shared understanding, which is established through meaningful and nonarbitrary actions taken by one or more persons (p. 254). This model has been applied to the analysis of the Arab Springs (Uhlaner, 2014), where participation is considered a means of gaining a sense of belonging and emotional connections (Donati, 2019). The main weaknesses of Uhlaner's theory are twofold: first, it views relational goods as the outcome of individual choices directed toward utility maximization, thereby ignoring their purely social character; and second, Uhlaner's theory aims to create a new category of goods that surpasses the shortcomings of orthodox utilitarianism, rather than deepening the notion of relational goods itself (Solci, 2009).

Donati's (1986) perspective, while partially consonant with Uhlaner's outlook, differs significantly in terms of the reasoning behind the genesis and preservation of relational goods. The scholar's supposition is grounded in relational sociology, in which relationships are seen as emergent realities, endowed with distinct properties and causal forces (Donati, 2019). Following this approach, relational goods cannot be reduced to subjective emotions or psychological states, nor to certain modes of communication with others; similarly, they are not generated by practicality or utility. Relational goods are social connections with their own ontological status, sought out for motives that go beyond utilitarian aims. Thus, the relational good is an emergent phenomenon arising from the interface between two or more people, who establish a network of relationships. Through these interactions, the parties attain advantages they could not otherwise acquire. Furthermore, not all relationships give rise to relational goods: Donati and Solci (2015) argue that these goods are the result of second-order social connections, in which, aside from the intersubjective relationship, another element—that of reflexivity—is also present.

Donati suggested that individuals should be interested in the relationship itself, which has intrinsic value to participants, regardless of its practical benefit. To conclude, both Gui and Uhlaner argue that relational good should not be seen as synonymous with a relationship, but rather as a result of it. Meanwhile, Nussbaum holds that relational good is the same as the relationship itself. Donati has proposed a more intricate definition that suggests that relational good is a result of behavior and is independent from the intentions of individuals. The combination of intersubjectivity and reflexivity allows for the formation of a space in which communication is encouraged and sustained.

2.3.1   Relational Goods: A Sense-Making Point of View

Relational goods, which can be derived from intersubjective and reflective connections, have the capacity to generate a supportive atmosphere that facilitates the emergence of various advantages. Such non-instrumental social ties can promote mutual learning between individuals and, consequently, increase the level of sense-making. Weick et al. (2008) have noted that sense-making is a cognitive process that allows the active subject to generate meaning by organizing the flow of experience. Through this process, the individual is able to continually assign meaning to their work and activity in the organization, resulting in ordered, generative, and meaningful experiences. The concept of sense-making is closely linked to praxis, which is a cycle of continuous interpretation and reinterpretation (Pellegrini et al., 2021). Further research shows that the sense-making process initially occurs at an individual level and then collectively. Therefore, the sense-making process is seen as a dynamic interplay between individual and collective levels. The transition from the individual to collective sense-making occurs through cycles of sense-making-sense-giving, indicating the interdependence between entities through reciprocal feedback exchange (Reflexive-Sensegiving; Robert & Ola, 2021). These cycles are not only sequential but also simultaneous and rely on the emotional and cognitive contagion occurring between organizational agents. Maitlis and Christianson (2014) and Sandberg and Tsoukas (2015) have demonstrated how the meaning-making process is initiated by identities and how this is affected by the social and contextual environment in which it takes place. Consequently, it can be argued that, in organizational contexts, relational goods (i.e., intersubjectivity and reflexivity) can promote sense-making processes because they contain identarian and generative elements. The reflective aspect of the relationship, in particular, allows us to acknowledge the differences between the individuals involved in the relationship, thereby leading to mutual growth. The sense-making process can also be seen as a form of collective learning, which we can refer to as "social learning." Social learning is a process of knowledge sharing through interactions between individuals or groups, which may involve learning from others, informing others, or both. Social learning can occur through direct interactions, such as conversations, or through indirect interactions, such as observing others. Furthermore, each individual can expand their perspective on the issue and learn from others' experiences. Thus, relational goods can provide a supportive atmosphere for social learning, allowing individuals to exchange knowledge and experiences and gain insights from one another. In addition, it can enable individuals to develop their own understanding of the situation and make more informed decisions. As such, relational goods can be seen as an important factor in promoting collective learning and sense-making, which can ultimately lead to increased organizational effectiveness.

2.3.2 Relational Goods to Generate Sense Within Organizations

In order to facilitate sense-making within organizations, relationships between individuals have emerged as essential. A strand of literature on sense-making suggests that groups of people generally tend to perceive and comprehend actions and events in similar ways (Smircich & Morgan, 1982). Meaning is thus collective, and organizations become networks of intersubjectively shared meanings (Brown et al., 2008). Ensuring a set of shared meanings is essential for an organization: this makes it easier to govern and manage employees and new organizational dynamics.

Employees, in order to develop similar meanings, need to be able to relate to one another: social relationships thus become important in business contexts. In fact, managers should strive to encourage relationships between employees for at least two reasons: first, groups of people who relate to one another develop similar meanings; second, the development of similar meanings might be a necessary condition for the success of work transformation situations. Following this perspective, Ahn and Hong (2019) examined the process through which individual knowledge is transformed into organizational knowledge, clarifying the sense-making process and demonstrating how learning for generating organizational knowledge depends on participation and communication and requires voluntary interactions based on intersubjectivity among members of the organization. This aspect of intersubjectivity is embedded within the broader notion of relational good. In sum, when organizations promote relationships aimed at personal growth, promote mutual education, and avoid the development of instrumental and shallow relationships, they can create an environment conducive to sense-making. Relational goods are valuable tools to help organizations reach their goals, as people together can achieve more than they could as individuals. They fulfill an essential role in organizational sense-making, as they contribute to a shared under-standing of the organization and its objectives. Relational goods are thus an essential part of the cognitive framework which supports individuals to make sense of their environment, understand their roles and responsibilities, and develop trust in the organization. The communicative arena created by intersubjective and reflexive relationships can also enable the exchange of information and experiences that lead to more effective decision-making and collaboration. Finally, they create a sense of belonging within the organization, which can increase productivity and morale. When organizations provide opportunities for the development of intersubjective and reflexive relationships among their employees, values and purposes are created. Moreover, this shared understanding is essential for the development of collective intelligence, as it allows individuals to coordinate and share their ideas, experiences, and perspectives. This trust-based culture can help to facilitate the exchange of knowledge and expertise, which can lead to more effective problem-solving and better decision-making.

REFERENCES

Ahn, J., & Hong, A. J. (2019). Transforming I into we in organizational knowledge creation: A case study. *Human Resource Development Quarterly, 30*(4), 565–582.

Barone, A. (2006). *Il diritto del rischio* (Vol. 2). Giuffrè Editore.

Becchetti, L., Pelloni, A., & Rossetti, F. (2008). Relational goods, sociability, and happiness. *Kyklos, 61*(3), 343–363.

Bénabou, R., & Tirole, J. (2006). Incentives and prosocial behavior. *American Economic Review, 96*(5), 1652–1678.

Bonelli, M., & Masi, F. G. (2011). *Studi sulle Categorie di Aristotele* (Vol. 61). Hakkert.

Borzaga, C., & Depedri, S. (2005). Interpersonal relations and job satisfaction: Some empirical results in social and community care services. In B. Gui & R. Sugden (Eds.), *Economics and social interaction: Accounting for interpersonal relations* (pp. 132–153). Cambridge University Press.

Brammer, S., Branicki, L., & Linnenluecke, M. K. (2020). COVID-19, societalization, and the future of business in society. *Academy of Management Perspectives, 34*(4), 493–507.

Brown, A. D., Stacey, P., & Nandhakumar, J. (2008). Making sense of sensemaking narratives. *Human Relations, 61*(8), 1035–1062.

Coelho, N. E., Jr., & Figueiredo, L. C. (2003). Patterns of intersubjectivity in the constitution of subjectivity: *Dimensions of otherness. Culture & Psychology, 9*(3), 193–208.

Cortella, L. (1996). La teoria critica della dialettica alla dialogica. *Fenomenologia e società, 20*(1–2), 210–230.

Crespi, F. (2004). *Identità E Riconoscimento Nella Sociologia Contemporanea*. Laterza.

Doherty, M. (2008). *Theory of mind: How children understand others' thoughts and feelings*. Psychology press.

Donati, P. (1986). *Introduzione alla sociologia relazionale*. Milano: Angeli.

Donati, P. (2014). Relational goods and their subjects: The ferment of a new civil society and civil democracy. *Recerca: Revista de pensament i anàlisi*, (14), 19–46.

Donati, P. (2016). L'enigma della relazione e la matrice teologica della società. In P. Donati, A. Malo, & G. Maspero (Eds.), *La vita come relazione. Un dialogo fra teologia, filosofia e scienze sociali*. Edizioni Santa Croce.

Donati, P. (2019). *Scoprire i beni relazionali*. Per generare una nuova socialità. Soveria Mannelli: Rubbettino.

Donati, P., & Solci, R. (2011). *I beni relazionali: che cosa sono e quali effetti producono*. Bollati Boringhieri.

Donati, P., & Solci, R. (2015). Misurare l'immateriale: il caso dei beni relazionali. *Sociologia e Ricerca Sociale, 108*(3), 13–32.

Donthu, N., & Gustafsson, A. (2020). Effects of COVID-19 on business and research. *Journal of Business Research, 117*, 284–289.

Greene, M. (1995). Teaching for openings. In *Releasing the imagination. Essays on education, the arts and social change* (pp. 109–121). Jossey-Bass Publishers.

Grootaert, C., & Van Bastelaer, T. (Eds.). (2002). *Understanding and measuring social capital: A multidisciplinary tool for practitioners (Vol. 1)*. World Bank Publications.

Gui, B. (1987). Eléments pour une définition d'économie communautaire. *Notes et Documents, 19/20*, 32–42.

Gui, B. (2005). From transactions to encounters: The joint generation of relational goods and conventional values. In B. Gui & R. Sugden (Eds.), *Economics and social interaction: Accounting for interpersonal relations* (pp. 23–51). Cambridge University Press.

Guiso, L., Sapienza, P., & Zingales, L. (2004). The role of social capital in financial development. *American Economic Review, 94*(3), 526–556.

Maitlis, S., & Christianson, M. (2014). Sensemaking in organizations: Taking stock and moving forward. *Academy of Management Annals, 8*(1), 57–125.

Maritain, J. (1947). *La personne et le bien commun*. Brouwer.

Marrucci, A., Ciappei, C., Zollo, L., & Rialti, R. (2022). Relational ontology for an ethics of work relationships. In *Philosophy and business ethics: Organizations, CSR and moral practice* (pp. 301–326). Springer International Publishing.

Marrucci, A., Rialti, R., Zollo, L., & Ciappei, C. (2020). Relational goods between person, acknowledgment and affective commitment: A contribution to the creation of public value. In *Grand challenges: Companies and universities working for a better society* (pp. 431–436). University of Pisa.

McClure, E. S., Vasudevan, P., Bailey, Z., Patel, S., & Robinson, W. R. (2020). Racial capitalism within public health—How occupational settings drive COVID-19 disparities. *American Journal of Epidemiology, 189*(11), 1244–1253.

Mori, J., & Hayashi, M. (2006). The achievement of intersubjectivity through embodied completions: A study of interactions between first and second language speakers. *Applied linguistics, 27*(2), 195–219.

Nussbaum, M. C. (1996). *La fragilità del bene: fortuna ed etica nella tragedia e nella filosofia greca*. Il Mulino, Bologna.

Pellegrini, M. M., Ciappei, C., Marzi, G., Dabić, M., & Egri, C. P. (2021). A philosophical approach to entrepreneurship education: A model based on Kantian and Aristotelian thought. *International Journal of Entrepreneurship and Small Business, 42*(1–2), 203–231.

Robert, K., & Ola, L. (2021). Reflexive sensegiving: An open-ended process of influencing the sensemaking of others during organizational change. *European Management Journal, 39*(4), 476–486.

Rossitto, C. (1993). LA DIALETTICA E IL SUO RUOLO NELLA "METAFISICA" DI ARISTOTELE. *Rivista di Filosofia neo-scolastica, 85*(2/4), 370–424.

Routledge, B. R., & Von Amsberg, J. (2003). Social capital and growth. *Journal of Monetary Economics, 50*(1), 167–193.

Sandberg, J., & Tsoukas, H. (2015). Making sense of the sensemaking perspective: Its constituents, limitations, and opportunities for further development. *Journal of Organizational Behavior, 36*(S1), S6–S32.

Sandywell, B. (2013). *Reflexivity and the crisis of Western reason: Logological investigations: Volume one.* Routledge.

Smircich, L., & Morgan, G. (1982). Leadership: The management of meaning. *The Journal of Applied Behavioral Science, 18*(3), 257–273.

Smith, D. W. (2005). The concept of the simulacrum: Deleuze and the overturning of Platonism. *Continental Philosophy Review, 38*(1–2), 89–123.

Solci, R. (2009). *I beni relazionali nella ricerca sociologica. Che cosa sono e quali effetti producono.* Tesi di Dottorato di ricerca sociologica, Università di Bologna, Dipartimento di Sociologia.

Uhlaner, C. J. (1989). Relational goods and participation: Incorporating sociability into a theory of rational action. *Public Choice, 62*(3), 253–285.

Uhlaner, C. J. (2014). Relational goods and resolving the paradox of political participation. *Recerca: revista de pensament i anàlisi, 14*, 47–72.

Weick, K. E., Sutcliffe, K. M., & Obstfeld, D. (2008). Organizing for high reliability: Processes of collective mindfulness. *Crisis Management, 3*(1), 81–123.

Zamagni, S. (2006). L'economia come se la persona contasse: verso una teoria economica relazionale. *Teoria economica e relazioni interpersonali*, 17–51.

Zamagni, S. (2008). Reciprocity, civil economy, common good. In *Pursuing the common good: How solidarity and subsidiarity can work together* (pp. 467–502). The Pontifical Academy of Social Sciences.

Zinkin, L., & Brown, D. (Eds.). (1996). *La psiche e il mondo sociale: La gruppoanalisi come strumento del cambiamento sociale.* Cortina.

CHAPTER 3

Relational Goods and Organization Change in 4.0 Era

Abstract Relational goods may play a role also in digital transformation projects. In particular, it has widely been observed how employee's engagement is fundamental to successfully digitally transform any business. In such a regard, it is relevant to unpack how these goods may arouse and how they may interrelate with the building blocks of digital transformation in 4.0. The analysis will focus on SMEs; indeed, this typology of business is the most diffused in any national economy. Likewise, SMEs are the business which most frequently experience difficulties in embracing opportunities deriving from digitalization.

Keywords Relational goods • Industry 4.0 • Digitalization • Digital transformation • Technology strategy • Digital humanism

3.1 The Importance of Relational Goods to Drive Organizational Change

Nowadays, most businesses are required to adopt digital technologies in order to respond to the increasing complexity of the environment. For instance, emergencies such as the COVID-19 pandemic and the 2021 Suez Canal Blockage necessitate that businesses become self-reliant and adaptive (Bartsch et al., 2020). These circumstances have favored the expansion and application of digital technologies which help organizations

A. Marrucci, R. Rialti, *Successful Digital Transformation Initiatives in SMEs*, https://doi.org/10.1007/978-3-031-36465-5_3

to automate processes while reducing the use of resources (Dimke et al., 2020). Moreover, digital technologies are also related to improved monitoring and standardized production in mass production processes, leading to greater efficiency and pursuit of quality (Jung et al., 2017). Moreover, with the growth in the availability of high-speed internet, interconnect machines, and fiscal advantages of 4.0 technologies in employees' places, many businesses are embracing digital technologies to become 4.0 compliant, which often involves replacing handmade work with automatic processes (Cugno et al., 2021). This phenomenon can be seen in industries such as IT components, computer productions, or automotive, which are shifting from partly to fully automatic 24/7 production processes.

Technological progress has become a powerful driver in shaping the future of our society, as it has completely reshaped and permeated the economic and social fields (Pham et al., 2020). The transition from the real to the virtual world has become a global trend, providing numerous opportunities for wealth creation (Nižetić et al., 2019). In particular, the digital transition will foster the discovery and implementation of increasingly smart solutions.

A smart element is defined as an object in which different fields of application that were previously separated are now interconnected, thanks to technologies. In the economic and managerial sphere, the smart concept has been studied in the manufacturing industry, where sensors, cloud computing, and big data enable the linking of different assets across companies and their integration into value networks (Stornelli et al., 2021). This new paradigm is based on the adoption of digital technologies for collecting and analyzing data in real time, profiling a possible target customer, and providing useful information to the production and logistics system. Furthermore, the presence of collaborative robots, virtual and augmented reality, allows for remote monitoring and control (Hirsch-Kreinsen, 2016). The massification of the technologies and applications has allowed even smaller businesses to become "smart" (Rialti et al., 2020).

Research suggests that technological changes will improve the quality of life by creating new opportunities and experiences (Dalenogare et al., 2018). On the other hand, some academics argue that technological revolutions will profoundly change the way we live, work, and relate (Burgess & Connell, 2020). One of the main concerns regarding I4.0 is the loss of jobs and excessive automation, which might lead to considering work as a tool and not as a human being purpose (Caruso, 2018). Automated factories may need slightly less labor, leading to mass poverty, unemployment, and inequality (Schwab, 2017). Moreover, some academics view it as a response to pervasive capitalism (Caruso, 2018).

Despite the potential employment consequences of I4.0, most research agrees that integrating digital technologies into human labor can lead to a more inclusive labor future (Caruso, 2018). This means that individuals should be the ones driving technologies, rather than the other way around. Valuing humans in the 4.0 technology paradigm is essential for the promotion and preservation of human flourishing and work dignity (Doolin & McLeod, 2007). In this process, the continuous creation of meaning is central to humanist business management: during contexts of technological transformation, it is essential to preserve human flourishing and protect identities (Roszkowska & Melé, 2021). In order to promote employees' support toward a digital transformation and rebalance their work and social identities, managers should implement strategies that recognize the employees' identities (Hecklau et al., 2016) since work allows people to define themselves.

Failure to recognize one's identity due to organizational and technological change may threaten the creation of meaning and human growth (Slater et al., 2016).

It has been argued that a working relationality that goes beyond the instrumental sphere can be used to foster the identity and meaning-generating activities of individuals within an organization. This is encapsulated by the concept of relational goods, which holds that intersubjective and self-reflexive relationships can further personal growth and mutual learning, thereby creating a generative environment. We suggest that the establishment of such relationships within an organization can create a communicative and learning-oriented space that is conducive to change. Thus, relational goods can be leveraged to facilitate digital transformation.

3.2   How Could Relational Goods Help Managers During Digital Transformation? A Humanistic Management Perspective

Humanism is a philosophical approach emphasizing the importance of the individual, free will, and the pursuit of happiness. It places the needs and interests of people at the center of the analysis (Aktouf, 1992). Approaching a research topic building on humanism thus requires us to focus on human behavior, human relationships, and human free will with regard to contingencies emerging in the environment (Melé, 2016).

In today's world, many of the decisions we make, from the technology we use to the ways we think and act, need to be explored through the lens of humanism (Koon, 2021).

Consistently, the importance of humanism in technology strategy is becoming increasingly apparent. As technology continues to evolve, it is becoming more and more intertwined with our lives and the ways in which we think and act (Jasanoff, 2016). Decisions regarding technology must thereby be kept up to date through continuous efforts to determine how technology affects people. By placing human needs and interests at the center of our decision-making, we can ensure that technology is used in a way that is beneficial to people and their lives (Acevedo, 2012).

Even in a business context, these considerations are becoming more and more important. Managers need to determine the degree to which technology is affecting their employees' lives and career perspectives in the long run (Daley, 1986).

Building on these premises, it is important to debate the importance of humanism in technology strategy. Humanistic approaches can be used to inform the development of technology, how it shapes the ways in which technology is used, and the ethical considerations that should be taken into account when using technology. The exploration should also consider how humanism can be used to create a more equitable and just environment within businesses (Aktouf, 1992).

With this in mind, the starting point of the analysis concerns the fact that the development of technology is a complex and multi-faceted process. It involves the collaboration of people from a variety of diverse backgrounds, and it is often informed by the latest scientific research. However, it is important to remember that technology is created for people (Rapp, 1985).

The most effective way to do this is to ensure that human needs and interests are taken into account when developing technology (Pirson & Lawrence, 2010). The technology should hence be designed with the user in mind, and it should be created in such a way that allows users to interact with it in a meaningful and enjoyable way.

Thus, in technological development, it is important to consider how this will be used by people, and to ensure that the technology is being used in a responsible while purposeful manner (Raikov, 2018). It is then relevant to take into account the potential risks associated with the use of the technology and ensure that these risks are minimized. It also means considering how the technology will be used and by whom, making sure that it is not used in a way that could be detrimental.

Once technology has been developed, it is important to consider how it will be used by people. It is fundamental to consider the potential benefits and harm associated with the use of the technology. When using technology, it is also important to evaluate the ethical implications of the technology. The potential impact of the technology on people's lives and whether or not it could be used in a way that is unethical or unjust is something managers should focus on during the technology strategy decisions (Fisk et al., 2019). Implications of the technology for society as a whole, to make sure that the technology is used in a way that is beneficial to society, have also to be gauged. Indeed, new technologies can have an enormous impact on society. Technology can be used to create a more equitable and just society, or it can be used to further inequality and injustice (Singh & Babbar, 2021).

Hereby, in the digital transformation process, it has been deemed relevant to root technological strategy on the seven core humanism principles (Geller, 2015), namely:

1. *Human dignity*: Respect and value the worth of every human being.
2. *Respect for autonomy*: Recognize and support individuals' right to make their own choices.
3. *Critical thinking*: Use reason and evidence to form judgments.
4. *Compassion and empathy*: Show understanding and kindness toward others.
5. *Equality and justice*: Treat all humans equally, regardless of race, gender, or other differences.
6. *Tolerance and acceptance*: Be open to different ideas and opinions.
7. *Self-reflection*: Reflect on your own beliefs and values to better understand yourself and the world around you.

In this way, managers can involve people in technology-orientated transformations. This approach considers employees as central to organizations, and technologies are then implemented around them and their needs, rather than with the purpose of replacing them (Daley, 1986).

With this in mind, as digital transformation continues to emerge as a need for businesses, strategies to integrate these principles in management will be explored. Specifically, the authors will consider the perspective of relational goods and their importance in SMEs.

3.2.1   *Transform to Survive: SMEs and I4.0*

SMEs are generally defined as any business with fewer than 250 employees and a turnover of less than €50 million. In Europe, SMEs account for more than 99% of all businesses and provide more than 60% of all employment. In Italy, SMEs account for around 98% of all businesses and provide around 45% of all employment (Hu et al., 2023).

SMEs are an essential part of the European and Italian economies. They are responsible for creating jobs, contributing to growth, and providing a wide range of services and products. SMEs are also an important source of innovation and are often the first to adopt new technologies and processes.

Despite these benefits, SMEs face a number of challenges. These include: a lack of access to finance, a lack of access to markets, and a lack of access to technology (Rialti et al., 2017). SMEs also face difficulty in navigating the complex regulatory and tax systems in Europe and Italy. These challenges can make it difficult for SMEs to remain competitive and profitable. Additionally, in recent years, SMEs have had limited access to new emerging technologies due to a lack of resources, capabilities, and skills (Marrucci et al., 2022, 2023).

However, the use of technology has become increasingly important for SMEs as they strive to remain competitive in a rapidly changing environment.

This phenomenon emerged as a dominant topic of research in the wake of the fourth industrial revolution (a.k.a. Industry 4.0). Industry 4.0 is the current trend of automation and data exchange in the manufacturing technologies (Guo et al., 2021). It is also linked to embedding the wide-ranging application of the Industrial Internet of Things (IIoT) or Smart Industry postulates. The concept of Industry 4.0 was first coined by the German government in 2011, with the aim of creating an environment of intelligent production systems (Xu et al., 2021).

Industry 4.0 is built on the idea of the Internet of Things (IoT), which is the concept of connecting devices to the internet in order to collect, exchange, and analyze data. In the context of Industry 4.0, this means that machines, devices, and sensors in a factory are connected to the internet, enabling them to communicate with each other and with other systems, such as computers and databases (Culot et al., 2019). This enables the factory to become a "smart factory," with the ability to optimize its performance and cost-effectiveness (Dalenogare et al., 2018).

Industry 4.0 has the potential to revolutionize the way businesses operate and produce goods and services (Rossit et al., 2019). The technology can enable businesses to increase efficiency, reduce costs, and improve customer satisfaction. The principal benefits that businesses (including SMEs) obtain as a consequence of the integration of Industry 4.0 technologies are as follows:

1. *Improved Efficiency*: By connecting machines and systems, businesses can eliminate the need for manual processes and manual data entry. This can reduce labor costs and increase efficiency.
2. *Increased Productivity*: By automating processes, businesses can reduce the amount of time needed to complete tasks and increase their output. This can lead to higher profits.
3. *Increased Quality*: By monitoring and analyzing data, businesses can quickly detect problems and take corrective action to ensure a high-quality product.
4. *Reduced Costs*: Automation can reduce labor costs, while data analysis can help businesses identify areas of waste and inefficiency, allowing them to reduce costs.
5. *Improved Customer Satisfaction*: By collecting data on customer behavior, businesses can better understand their needs and tailor their offerings accordingly.

The transformation toward Industry 4.0 is also dubbed as digital transformation, and this is made possible through a number of technologies (Marrucci et al., 2023), including:

1. *Sensors and Actuators*: Sensors are used to collect data from the environment and machines. This data can then be used to monitor performance and take corrective action. The tools undertaking these corrective actions are dubbed as actuators, and these are fundamental to transforming the electrical signal from a sensor into a real-world action.
2. *Robotics*: Robotics can be used to automate tasks such as material handling and assembly. This can reduce labor costs and increase productivity.

3. *Machine Learning and Big Data Analytics*: Machine learning algorithms can be used to analyze data and identify patterns that can be used to improve processes and products. Analysis methods based on machine learning are the foundation of Big Data Analytics, which are methodologies used to analyze large unstructured datasets.

4. *Cloud Computing*: Cloud computing provides the infrastructure needed to store and analyze data. It also allows for remote access and collaboration between teams.

5. *Augmented Reality and Virtual Reality*: Augmented reality can be used to provide workers with a detailed view of the workplace, allowing them to quickly identify and fix problems. Virtual reality, instead, allows them to create completely complementary worlds in which business and consumers may interact.

6. *Artificial Intelligence*: Machines in Industry 4.0 world may be endowed with Artificial Intelligence, allows these tools to make autonomous decisions (i.e., to auto-optimize production processes).

To remain competitive SMEs have to embrace these technologies and face their implementation in production processes as, in the past decade, the adoption of Industry 4.0 (i.e., the achievement of a complete digital transformation) has become an essential part of modern business (Rossit et al., 2019). It refers to the process of integrating digital technologies into all aspects of a business, from marketing and customer service to operations and product development (Guo et al., 2021). For these businesses, digital transformation is especially important, since it represents one of the only ways to remain competitive in respect of larger counterparts (Rialti et al., 2019). With digital transformation, SMEs can gain access to new technologies, streamline operations, and increase their competitive edge (Pirson et al., 2019).

Among the general benefits a business may achieve in relation to digital transformation, the three most relevant ones are efficiency, cost savings, and customer engagement (Marrucci et al., 2023).

In respect of efficiency, digital transformation can help SMEs streamline their operations, making them more efficient and productive. By leveraging digital technologies, SMEs can automate manual tasks, reduce errors, and improve workflows. This can result in a significant decrease in the time and effort required to complete tasks, freeing up resources for other projects. Digital transformation can also help SMEs save money. By automating tasks, businesses can reduce operational costs, such as labor and materials. Digital technologies can also help businesses save money on marketing and customer service by enabling them to reach customers more quickly and cost-effectively. Finally, digital transformation can also help SMEs better engage with customers. By leveraging digital technologies, businesses can more effectively communicate with customers, providing them with information, support, and feedback. Furthermore, digital technologies can help businesses gain valuable customer insights, allowing them to better understand customer needs and preferences. This can result in increased customer loyalty and improved customer satisfaction (Calluzzo & Cante, 2004).

Some side benefits may also be obtained, thanks to digital transformation. For example, Industry 4.0 technologies can help businesses to reduce their environmental impact. By using sensors, businesses can monitor their energy usage and identify ways to reduce their energy consumption. This could enable them to reduce their carbon emissions, which can have a positive impact on their reputation, helping them to develop a more sustainable business model. Furthermore, businesses may be able to use Industry 4.0 to develop new products and services. By collecting and analyzing data, businesses can identify new customer needs and develop products and services that meet those needs. This could enable them to stay ahead of the competition, attract new customers, and increase their profitability (Rialti et al., 2020).

Despite the potential benefits of Industry 4.0, the adoption of this plethora of technologies is neither easy nor immediate (Masood & Sonntag, 2020). With this in mind, SMEs may face the following barriers:

1. *Cost*: Adopting Industry 4.0 can be expensive as it requires the purchase of new technology and the training of staff.
2. *Security*: As Industry 4.0 involves connecting machines and systems to the internet, cyber-attacks present a real risk. Businesses must ensure their systems are secure.
3. *Compliance*: Depending on the industry, there may be legal and regulatory requirements that need to be met before adopting Industry 4.0.
4. *Skills*: Many businesses may not have the necessary skills to implement and use the technology effectively.
5. *Resistance to Change*: Change can be difficult, and many businesses may be reluctant to adopt new technologies.

The first three barriers can be overcome by SMEs through material resources. Costs, indeed, may be reduced or amortized through financing means and governmental incentive programs. Industria 4.0 law in Italy serves as a good example of this, offering tax breaks of up to 40% of the total investment in digital transformation. Compliance and security may likewise be addressed by managers through accurate legal assessments and the implementation of security compliant technologies. However, skills and resistance to change are not exclusively solved through money and incentives. It is extremely important to consider the fact that skills may stem from training programs that seek to reinforce the competencies of the workforce. Employees could still be resistant to new technologies, as they may be with regard to any form of change. Even in the presence of training programs, staff could wish to maintain their working methods, thus preventing them from accepting new methods as a result of their personal approaches.

3.2.2   Overcoming Employee Resistance During Digital Transformation

Employees are typically resistant to change because it can create an uncertain environment, cause disruption to workflows, and require individuals to learn new processes and skills. Change can also challenge existing power dynamics and relationships within a workplace, which can cause the workforce to feel insecure and uneasy. This resistance may also be motivated by a fear of the unknown, as employees may not understand how the change will affect their job performance or their future prospects (Dalenogare et al., 2018).

In short, change often requires employees to step out of their comfort zone, which may be a difficult or uncomfortable thing for them to do (Horváth & Szabó, 2019). Likewise, change could create additional work for everyone, as employees are frequently accustomed to existing systems and processes and may not see the need for change or be willing to do something different in respect of what they have done in their careers so far (particularly for employees approaching retirement age).

In order to successfully implement change, managers must step up and address everyone else's concerns, ensuring that they understand the need for the change, the benefits it will bring, and how it will improve their job performance. Managers, through company-wide programs, should also ensure they provide the necessary resources and training to enable employees to successfully adapt to new processes and systems. Flexibility, in respect of original plans and openness to feedback and suggestions, is likewise fundamental, as it can help to foster trust and open communication between employees and management (Rialti et al., 2020).

In the context of the digital transformation caused by Industry 4.0, change is often challenged by employees, as technology requires them to change the way they have always worked.

This notwithstanding, it is undeniable that technology has become an integral part of the modern workplace, and most businesses rely on technology to some extent. Understanding the reasons behind employee resistance is key to developing effective strategies to overcome it. In this vein, it is relevant to focus on which actions could be performed by managers to overcome this resistance (Tavares et al., 2022). Nowadays, the most consolidate strategies to overcome resistance are: effective communication, training and support, creating a sense of ownership, and offering incentives.

Effective Communication
One of the most important strategies for overcoming employees' resistance to technology adoption is effective communication. It is essential that managers clearly explain the reasons behind their introduction of the new technology and how it will benefit both the organization and its employees. This should include a thorough explanation of the specific features of the new technology and how it will help employees in their work (Elshof & Hendrawan, 2022). Additionally, it is important to provide employees with ample opportunity to ask questions and express concerns. Informed employees are more likely to accept new technology. The development of feedback mechanisms to collect insights and knowledge from employees is therefore fundamental. This knowledge has to be categorized according to salient and emergent topics capable of aiding the transformation process and making employees feel included.

Additionally, employees should be presented with technological roadmaps to show them the direction in which the business should go according to the new technologies. These kinds of maps may help incorporate technologies into the vision of the company more fully, thus fostering their acceptance (Green, 2021).

For Industry 4.0 technologies, such as AI and robotics, involving employees in the implementation process is fundamental in encouraging them accept the technologies. Employers should involve employees in the selection of AI and robots, as well as in the planning and implementation of any initiatives. This can help to ensure that decisions that are made are in line with the needs and concerns of employees (Bachmann et al., 2018).

Training and Support

Training and support are both essential when attempting to overcome employees' resistance to technology adoption. Employees need to feel confident in their ability to use the new technology effectively. Providing adequate training and offering ongoing support can help to make sure that employees feel comfortable and are capable of using the new technology (Masood & Sonntag, 2020). Manuals, tutorials, and troubleshooting tips should be provided, and if employees know that they have someone to turn to if they have any questions or issues, they will be more likely to accept the new technology (Davila & Elvira, 2012).

These practices are particularly useful in instances where the technologies to be implemented are particularly complex and sometimes controversial (i.e., they may replace humans in the workplace). For example, many employees may be wary of AI and robots because they do not understand how to use them or how they can help them in their jobs. Training and support can help to make staff more comfortable with the use of AI and robots in the workplace (Carabantes, 2021). Training should cover the basics of how AI and robots work and how they can be used to help employees in their roles (Winkelhaus et al., 2022). Support should also be provided to help employees understand how to use technology and how to troubleshoot any issues that may arise.

Creating a Sense of Ownership

Creating a sense of ownership in the new technology is another important strategy for overcoming employee resistance. This can involve including employees in the decision-making process or giving them an opportunity to provide feedback and offer suggestions (Bachmann et al., 2018). Additionally, allowing employees to customize the technology to suit their individual needs can help make them feel more invested in the new system. By giving employees a sense of ownership, they will be more likely to accept and embrace the new technology.

With this in mind, a strategy which could be relevant is the identification of transformation champions. Transformation champions are employees that act as intermediate figures between managers and the rest of the workforce, their roles can be reassumed in the providing and collection of feedbacks, and as fosterers of motivations. Specifically, they collect information from others and communicate these thoughts to leaders (Calluzzo & Cante, 2004). Transformation leaders can be selected according to their skills, and they can be entrusted with part of the project, making them effectively project owners (Waddock, 2016).

Offering Incentives

Offering incentives for using the new technology is a great way to motivate employees to adopt it. Examples of incentives include bonuses, rewards, and recognition for those who successfully use the new technology. This can help build enthusiasm and commitment to the new system, which can go a long way when it comes to increasing acceptance (Winkelhaus et al., 2022).

The best way to assuage technology-derived fears is by offering employees career development opportunities. This can include providing training in new skills that are needed to work with, for example, AI, or offering job retraining for employees who may be displaced. Employers should also provide career guidance and counselling to help employees transition into new roles (Bosman et al., 2020).

Cultivate a Collaborative Culture

Finally, managers should work to create a collaborative culture in the workplace. They have thus to encourage employees to work together to identify ways to use technologies and robots to improve processes, increase efficiency, and reduce individual workloads (Carabantes, 2021). Employers should also create an environment in which employees feel comfortable asking questions and voicing their concerns about specific technologies (Tavares et al., 2022). This can help to foster an atmosphere of trust and acceptance, ultimately leading to improved employee morale.

With these actions in mind, it may be possible for SMEs to achieve digital transformation through employee involvement. However, all these actions link back to one factor, which needs to be considered: leadership. Managers (the people leading the business) need to adapt along with the company. It is not possible for us to think about the digital transformation process without thinking about the need for leaders to change (Kohles et al., 2013).

In this regard, transformational leadership is important to the process of digital transformation, as it focuses on collaboration between personnel and the development of a shared vision with regard to the organization's future (Waddock, 2016).

Transformational leadership is a style of leadership that focuses on inspiring and motivating team members to achieve a common goal. Transformational leaders emphasize collaboration and the development of a shared vision for the organization's future (Kohles et al., 2013). This style of leadership is based on the concept of "servant leadership," which is the idea of leading from a position of service, rather than from a position of power. Transformational leaders are focused on creating a culture of trust, respect, and collaboration within the organization, as expected within the transformational processes (Chang, 2002). They have the ability to motivate and inspire employees, and they are able to communicate a clear vision of the organization's future. Transformational leaders also emphasize innovation and risk-taking, which can be important to the transformation processes.

Following a transformational leadership style may lead to many diverse benefits throughout the process of digital transformation. For example, by sharing their vision and the transformation process, transformational leaders can help to ensure that everyone within the organization is on the same page and that all stakeholders are working together to make the transformation a success (AlNuaimi et al., 2022). Transformational leadership also gives a sense of leadership and direction to the organization. Digital transformation is a complex process, and it can be difficult for an organization to know which direction to take. Transformational leaders can provide clarity and direction, which can help to ensure that the organization is taking the right steps toward digital transformation.

While the process of digital transformation can be complex and challenging, it is possible to successfully implement this in practice through a transformational approach. The first step is to develop a clear understanding of the organization's goals and objectives. This will help to ensure that everyone is working toward the same goal and that the organization is taking steps in the right direction. Once a shared vision has been established, it is important to create a culture of collaboration within the organization (Ardi et al., 2020). Transformational leaders can help to ensure that team members are working together and that everyone is motivated to work toward a common goal. Then, transformational leaders can help to create a culture of innovation and risk-taking, which are essential to the process of digital transformation. Transformational leaders are more prone to jointly evaluate the outcomes of a project together with employees, thus fostering the mutual exchange of information (Hirman et al., 2019).

This notwithstanding, even a transformational leadership approach can have some pitfalls in its application. For example, scholars have observed how transformational leaders are often still hands-off with regard to the practical tasks that need to be performed on a daily basis. These individuals will still act as detached leaders, while they promote involvement from everyone. In this vein, we have observed how transformational leaders frequently induce anxiety in collaborators, as they are seen as "perfect" by everyone else outside of the transformation project but are still considered too removed from reality for those directly involved in the project (Porfirio et al., 2021). Additionally, the confrontation time between the people involved in the project has been seen as something that could potentially be harmful, as some people may feel afraid to report failures. This occurrence may be related to the fact that some transformational leaders are not eager to own up to their own mistakes and failures (Davila & Elvira, 2012).

In this regard, research and practice need to focus on the central point in any business, namely, the relationship between employees and between staff and leaders. This approach aligns with the postulates of humanistic management and may allow staff to overcome the limitations of transformational leadership (Acevedo, 2012). According to internal systemic views of businesses, organizations are bundles of relationships, and when one of these relationships is changing, the equilibrium within the business needs to change accordingly (Roszkowska & Melé, 2021).

Relational goods may then emerge as a suitable approach with which to manage tensions existing within the business.

3.2.3   Relational Goods and Digital Transformation

Technological change processes may bring out situations of skepticism in employees due to the threat of no longer recognizing themselves within the workplace, losing social and personal identity. Some scholars of organization and strategic change have recognized that in innovation processes a fundamental role is played by the individuals involved in the change process (Amis et al., 2004; Huy et al., 2014). According to these studies, changes alter the power structure, culture, and baselines of the organization, highlighting a very critical scenario. Precisely because the introduction of a new initiative impacts a multiplicity of dynamics, it would be insufficient to focus the debate on how the employee might use the new technologies, that is, on implementation alone. Indeed, this perspective might create an imbalance between comprehension and implementation of change processes (Jiao & Zhao, 2014). Because implementation is one of the most critical dimensions within a broader change process, efforts should also focus on the steps preceding implementation itself.

To avoid these issues, we argue that the organization should promote the development of appropriate communication arenas that go beyond the mere instrumental sphere. In this way, despite changes in technology, the enterprise could remain a people-oriented, ethical, and relationship-oriented place (Ashforth et al., 2020). Giving value to intersubjective and reflexive relationships allows employees to rediscover their self-esteem, preventing inertia to change.

The development of intersubjective and reflexive relationships can lead to the generation of relational goods, which are intangible benefits deriving from the establishment of relationships between individuals or entities. Examples of such relational goods include trust, commitment, and loyalty (Donati, 2019). As these non-instrumental relationships foster commitment and trust between employees and organizations, they can facilitate digital transformation processes by providing a communicative vehicle through which positive effects can be produced. High levels of trust may result in the successful introduction of new technologies and processes. Furthermore, the strengthening of work relationality can produce a more positive work environment, leading to heightened productivity and a better experience for employees.

To sum, relational goods are essential for any digital transformation initiative because they provide the foundation for successful change. They promote trust and collaboration between employees, which helps to create a positive workplace culture. Furthermore, they enable effective communication, mutual and meaningful understanding between team members, which helps to ensure that the initiative is successful.

REFERENCES

Acevedo, A. (2012). Personalist business ethics and humanistic management: Insights from Jacques Maritain. *Journal of Business Ethics, 105*, 197–219.

Aktouf, O. (1992). Management and theories of organizations in the 1990s: Toward a critical radical humanism? *Academy of Management Review, 17*(3), 407–431.

AlNuaimi, B. K., Singh, S. K., Ren, S., Budhwar, P., & Vorobyev, D. (2022). Mastering digital transformation: The nexus between leadership, agility, and digital strategy. *Journal of Business Research, 145*, 636–648.

Amis, J., Slack, T., & Hinings, C. R. (2004). The pace, sequence, and linearity of radical change. *Academy of Management Journal, 47*(1), 15–39.

Ardi, A., Djati, S. P., Bernarto, I., Sudibjo, N., Yulianeu, A., Nanda, H. A., & Nanda, K. A. (2020). The relationship between digital transformational leadership styles and knowledge-based empowering interaction for increasing organisational innovativeness. *International Journal of Innovation, Creativity and Change, 11*(3), 259–277.

Ashforth, B. E., Schinoff, B. S., & Brickson, S. L. (2020). "My company is friendly," "Mine'sa Rebel": Anthropomorphism and shifting organizational identity from "What" to "Who". *Academy of Management Review, 45*(1), 29–57.

Bachmann, C., Sasse, L., & Habisch, A. (2018). Applying the practical wisdom lenses in decision-making: An integrative approach to humanistic management. *Humanistic Management Journal, 2*, 125–150.

Bartsch, S., Weber, E., Büttgen, M., & Huber, A. (2020). Leadership matters in crisis-induced digital transformation: How to lead service employees effectively during the COVID-19 pandemic. *Journal of Service Management, 31*(1), 71–85.

Bosman, L., Hartman, N., & Sutherland, J. (2020). How manufacturing firm characteristics can influence decision making for investing in Industry 4.0 technologies. *Journal of Manufacturing Technology Management, 31*(5), 1117–1141.

Burgess, J., & Connell, J. (2020). New technology and work: Exploring the challenges. *The Economic and Labour Relations Review, 31*(3), 310–323.

Calluzzo, V. J., & Cante, C. J. (2004). Ethics in information technology and software use. *Journal of Business Ethics, 51*, 301–312.

Carabantes, M. (2021). Smart socio-technical environments: A paternalistic and humanistic management proposal. *Philosophy & Technology, 34*(4), 1531–1544.

Caruso, L. (2018). Digital innovation and the fourth industrial revolution: Epochal social changes? *AI & Society, 33*(3), 379–392.

Chang, O. (2002). Humanistic Buddhism and knowledge management. *Hsi Lai Journal of Humanistic Buddhism= 西來人間佛教學報, 3*, 227–243.

Cugno, M., Castagnoli, R., & Büchi, G. (2021). Openness to Industry 4.0 and performance: The impact of barriers and incentives. *Technological Forecasting and Social Change, 168*. https://doi.org/10.1016/j.techfore.2021.120756

Culot, G., Fattori, F., Podrecca, M., & Sartor, M. (2019). Addressing Industry 4.0 cybersecurity challenges. *IEEE Engineering Management Review, 47*(3), 79–86.

Dalenogare, L. S., Benitez, G. B., Ayala, N. F., & Frank, A. G. (2018). The expected contribution of Industry 4.0 technologies for industrial performance. *International Journal of Production Economics, 204*, 383–394.

Daley, D. M. (1986). Humanistic management and organizational success: The effect of job and work environment characteristics on organizational effectiveness, public responsiveness, and job satisfaction. *Public Personnel Management, 15*(2), 131–142.

Davila, A., & Elvira, M. M. (2012). Humanistic leadership: Lessons from Latin America. *Journal of World Business, 47*(4), 548–554.

Dimke, C., Lee, M. C., & Bayham, J. (2020). Working from a distance: Who can afford to stay home during COVID-19? Evidence from mobile device data. *medRxiv.* https://doi.org/10.1101/2020.07.20.20153577

Donati, P. (2019). *Scoprire i beni relazionali. Per generare una nuova socialità.* Soveria Mannelli.

Doolin, B., & McLeod, L. (2007). Information technology at work: The implications for dignity at work. In *Dimensions of dignity at work* (pp. 174–195). Routledge.

Elshof, M., & Hendrawan, B. (2022). Humanistic communication professionals: Dialogue and listening skills as core competencies of humanistic communication professionals in the Netherlands. *Journal of Communication Management, 26*, 236–253.

Fisk, R., Fuessel, A., Laszlo, C., Struebi, P., Valera, A., & Weiss, C. (2019). Systemic social innovation: Co-creating a future where humans and all life thrive. *Humanistic Management Journal, 4*, 191–214.

Geller, E. S. (2015). Seven life lessons from humanistic behaviorism: How to bring the best out of yourself and others. *Journal of Organizational Behavior Management, 35*(1–2), 151–170.

Green, B. (2021). The contestation of tech ethics: A sociotechnical approach to technology ethics in practice. *Journal of Social Computing, 2*(3), 209–225.

Guo, D., Li, M., Lyu, Z., Kang, K., Wu, W., Zhong, R. Y., & Huang, G. Q. (2021). Synchroperation in Industry 4.0 manufacturing. *International Journal of Production Economics, 238*, 108171.

Hecklau, F., Galeitzke, M., Flachs, S., & Kohl, H. (2016). Holistic approach for human resource management in Industry 4.0. *Procedia Cirp, 54*, 1–6.

Hirman, M., Benesova, A., Steiner, F., & Tupa, J. (2019). Project management during the Industry 4.0 implementation with risk factor analysis. *Procedia Manufacturing, 38*, 1181–1188.

Hirsch-Kreinsen, H. (2016). Digitization of industrial work: Development paths and prospects. *Journal for Labour Market Research, 49*(1), 1–14.

Horváth, D., & Szabó, R. Z. (2019). Driving forces and barriers of Industry 4.0: Do multinational and small and medium-sized companies have equal opportunities? *Technological Forecasting and Social Change, 146*, 119–132.

Hu, L., Olivieri, M., & Rialti, R. (2023). Dynamically adapting to the new normal: Unpacking SMEs' adoption of social media during COVID-19 outbreaks. *Journal of Business & Industrial Marketing.* Forthcoming.

Huy, Q. N., Corley, K. G., & Kraatz, M. S. (2014). From support to mutiny: Shifting legitimacy judgments and emotional reactions impacting the implementation of radical change. *Academy of Management Journal, 57*(6), 1650–1680.

Jasanoff, S. (2016). *The ethics of invention: Technology and the human future.* W. W. Norton & Company.

Jiao, H., & Zhao, G. (2014). When will employees embrace managers' technological innovations? The mediating effects of employees' perceptions of fairness on their willingness to accept change and its legitimacy. *Journal of Product Innovation Management, 31*(4), 780–798.

Jung, K., Choi, S., Kulvatunyou, B., Cho, H., & Morris, K. C. (2017). A reference activity model for smart factory design and improvement. *Production Planning and Control, 28*(2), 108–122.

Kohles, J. C., Bligh, M. C., & Carsten, M. K. (2013). The vision integration process: Applying Rogers' diffusion of innovations theory to leader–follower communications. *Leadership, 9*(4), 466–485.

Koon, V. Y. (2021). Bibliometric analyses on the emergence and present growth of humanistic management. *International Journal of Ethics and Systems, 37*(4), 581–598.

Marrucci, A., Ciappei, C., Zollo, L., & Rialti, R. (2022). Relational ontology for an ethics of work relationships. In *Philosophy and business ethics: Organizations, CSR and moral practice* (pp. 301–326). Springer International Publishing.

Marrucci, A., Rialti, R., & Balzano, M. (2023). Exploring paths underlying Industry 4.0 implementation in manufacturing SMEs: A fuzzy-set qualitative comparative analysis. *Management Decision.* Forthcoming.

Masood, T., & Sonntag, P. (2020). Industry 4.0: Adoption challenges and benefits for SMEs. *Computers in Industry, 121,* 103261.

Melé, D. (2016). Understanding humanistic management. *Humanistic Management Journal, 1,* 33–55.

Nižetić, S., Djilali, N., Papadopoulos, A., & Rodrigues, J. J. (2019). Smart technologies for promotion of energy efficiency, utilization of sustainable resources and waste management. *Journal of Cleaner Production, 231,* 565–591.

Pham, N. M., Huynh, T. L. D., & Nasir, M. A. (2020). Environmental consequences of population, affluence and technological progress for European countries: A Malthusian view. *Journal of Environmental Management, 260,* 110143.

Pirson, M., Vázquez-Maguirre, M., Corus, C., Steckler, E., & Wicks, A. (2019). Dignity and the process of social innovation: Lessons from social entrepreneurship and transformative services for humanistic management. *Humanistic Management Journal, 4,* 125–153.

Pirson, M. A., & Lawrence, P. R. (2010). Humanism in business–towards a paradigm shift? *Journal of Business Ethics, 93,* 553–565.

Porfírio, J. A., Carrilho, T., Felício, J. A., & Jardim, J. (2021). Leadership characteristics and digital transformation. *Journal of Business Research, 124,* 610–619.

Raikov, A. (2018). Accelerating technology for self-organising networked democracy. *Futures, 103,* 17–26.

Rapp, F. (1985). Humanism and technology: The two-cultures debate. *Technology in Society, 7*(4), 423–435.

Rialti, R., Marzi, G., Caputo, A., & Mayah, K. A. (2020). Achieving strategic flexibility in the era of big data: The importance of knowledge management and ambidexterity. *Management Decision, 58*(8), 1585–1600.

Rialti, R., Pellegrini, M. M., Caputo, A., & Dabic, M. (2017). Entrepreneurial education and internationalisation of firms in transition economies: A conceptual framework from the case of Croatia. *World Review of Entrepreneurship, Management and Sustainable Development, 13*(2–3), 290–313.

Rialti, R., Zollo, L., Ferraris, A., & Alon, I. (2019). Big data analytics capabilities and performance: Evidence from a moderated multi-mediation model. *Technological Forecasting and Social Change, 149,* 119781.

Rossit, D. A., Tohmé, F., & Frutos, M. (2019). Industry 4.0: Smart scheduling. *International Journal of Production Research, 57*(12), 3802–3813.

Roszkowska, P., & Melé, D. (2021). Organizational factors in the individual ethical behaviour. The notion of the "organizational moral structure". *Humanistic Management Journal, 6,* 187–209.

Schwab, K. (2017). *The fourth industrial revolution.* Currency.

Singh, R. K., & Babbar, M. (2021). Religious diversity at workplace: A literature review. *Humanistic Management Journal, 6,* 229–247.

Slater, M. J., Evans, A. L., & Turner, M. J. (2016). Implementing a social identity approach for effective change management. *Journal of Change Management, 16*(1), 18–37.

Stornelli, A., Ozcan, S., & Simms, C. (2021). Advanced manufacturing technology adoption and innovation: A systematic literature review on barriers, enablers, and innovation types. *Research Policy, 50*(6), 104229.

Tavares, M. C., Azevedo, G., & Marques, R. P. (2022). The challenges and opportunities of Era 5.0 for a more humanistic and sustainable society—A literature review. *Societies, 12*(6), 149–170.

Waddock, S. (2016). Developing humanistic leadership education. *Humanistic Management Journal, 1,* 57–73.

Winkelhaus, S., Grosse, E. H., & Glock, C. H. (2022). Job satisfaction: An explorative study on work characteristics changes of employees in Intralogistics 4.0. *Journal of Business Logistics, 43*(3), 343–367.

Xu, X., Lu, Y., Vogel-Heuser, B., & Wang, L. (2021). Industry 4.0 and Industry 5.0—Inception, conception and perception. *Journal of Manufacturing Systems, 61,* 530–535.

CHAPTER 4

Including Relational Goods Within the Diffusion of Innovation Framework

Abstract Rogers' Diffusion of Innovation Theory (DOI) is a parsimonious theory to explore how a technology is adopted by a social group (including organizations). The DOI pertains that users may be dived within five categories: innovators, early adopters, early majority, late majority, and laggards. Four macro factors influence technology diffusion: social system, relative advantage, communication, and time. In such a regard, scant attention has traditionally been paid to communication and social system importance in technological diffusion within an organization, while these two factors may be the most relevant in Industry 4.0 oriented transformations. Building on this assumption, the authors attempt to contextualize how the two constituents of relational goods may be integrated within the DOI Theory.

Keywords Diffusion of innovation • Digital technologies • Digital innovation • Social system • Internal communication • Technological complexity

© The Author(s), under exclusive license to Springer Nature Switzerland AG 2023
A. Marrucci, R. Rialti, *Successful Digital Transformation Initiatives in SMEs*, https://doi.org/10.1007/978-3-031-36465-5_4

4.1   REVIEWING THE FOUR CORNERSTONES
UNDERPINNING THE DIFFUSION OF INNOVATION

For more than 20 years, the process of adopting new innovations has been studied, and one of the most widely used models is described by Rogers (2003) in his book *Diffusion of Innovations* (from now onward, the name of the theory, Diffusion of Innovation, will be referred to as DOI). Research from a range of disciplines, such as history, economics, technology, and education, has employed Rogers' theory as a framework. This theory is deemed to be one of the most suitable when it comes to examining the adoption of technology in heterogenous contexts (Zenko & Mulej, 2011). Rogers (2003) commonly referred to technology and innovation synonymously, considering technology to be "a design for instrumental action that reduces the uncertainty in the cause-effect relationships involved in achieving a desired outcome" (p. 13). Such a scheme comprises hardware, which is the physical embodiment of a specific technological innovation, and software, which is formed by the ensemble of codes making the technology work and the information base for the tool (p. 259). Usually, hardware is adopted more quickly than software. Hardware is more visible, while software needs to be accepted to be understood by users.

According to Rogers (2003), adoption is a decision about adopting an innovation, and rejection is instead a decision "not to adopt an innovation" (p. 177).

The theory thus provides insights into how a technological innovation can spread throughout a population spanning five distinct types of adopters: innovators, early adopters, early majority, late majority, and laggards. Each adopter category has its own characteristics, motivations, and behaviors that make them unique when it comes to adopting new ideas and products (Zhou, 2008). *Innovators* are the first category of adopters and are typically risk-takers and visionaries who embrace new ideas and products. They are willing to experiment with new ideas and are willing to accept the risks associated with them. Innovators are usually motivated by the desire to be first and to be seen as pioneers and trendsetters. They are usually highly educated, have financial resources and access to information, and are well networked. *Early adopters* make up the second category of adopters, and these are typically opinion leaders who are respected within their social network. They are typically well-educated, have financial resources, and are also highly networked. Early adopters are motivated by the desire to be seen as trendsetters and to be seen as forward-thinking and knowledgeable (Elmghaamez et al., 2022). They are usually willing to try out new products and services and are not as risk-averse as innovators. The *early majority* is the third category of adopters, typically made up of people who are well-educated and have access to resources (English, 2016). They are usually well-connected and have the ability to influence others in their social network. Early majority adopters are motivated by the desire to make good decisions and to be seen as knowledgeable and wise. They are typically more risk-averse than innovators and early adopters, and will wait until a product or service has been tested and proven before they adopt it. The *late majority* is the fourth category of adopters and this category is typically made up of people who are less educated, have fewer resources, and are less connected than the previous three categories. They are typically more conservative and risk-averse and tend to wait until a product or service has been proven and accepted by others before they adopt it. They are motivated by the desire to make a safe decision and to avoid any potential risks associated with a product or service (Zhu et al., 2012). The *laggards* are the last category of adopters, and these are typically made up of people who are very traditional in nature and are resistant to change. They are typically older and less educated and have fewer resources than individuals in the other categories. They are often the last to adopt technology and are usually motivated by the desire to remain with what is familiar and safe (Valente, 1996).

Diffusion is consistently the process by which "an innovation is communicated through certain channels over time among the members of a specific social system" within a population of potential users (Rogers, 2003, p.5).

Building on this definition, it is possible to identify the four leading cornerstones affecting the diffusion of innovation, namely, the *innovation* itself (the typology of innovation), *communication channels*, *time*, and *social systems* (Lundblad, 2003).

Innovation

According to Rogers (2003, p.12), *innovation* is an idea, practice, or project perceived as new by an individual or an organization. Even if the innovation itself is not necessarily new, if it is perceived to be new, then it can be considered an innovation. Uncertainty is a common obstacle when it comes to the adoption of innovation, as the consequences of adoption may be uncertain. To reduce this uncertainty, individuals should be informed of the advantages and disadvantages so that they can be aware of the consequences. Consequences can be classified as desirable or undesirable, direct or indirect, and anticipated or unanticipated.

The innovation-decision process is then made up of three steps: *knowledge*, *persuasion*, and *decision*. After these three steps, in case of adoption of technology, two more phases may follow *action* and *confirmation*.

As previously assessed, the innovation-decision process starts with the *knowledge* stage. During this time, the individual identifies a suitable possible technological solution with which to address his/her problems and start to seek information. They are likely to ask questions such as "What?", "How?", and "Why?" during this phase. The demand for knowledge can be divided into three different types: Awareness-knowledge, How-to-knowledge, and Principles-knowledge. Awareness-knowledge is the knowledge of the innovation's existence. This can motivate the individual to learn more and potentially adopt it. How-to-knowledge holds information on how to use the innovation correctly. This is an essential factor in the innovation-decision process. Principles-knowledge involves the functioning principles and assesses why the innovation works. While this knowledge is important, an individual's attitude can still lead to the adoption or rejection of the innovation.

The *persuasion* phase happens instead when the individual has a so-called *zero* attitude with regard to the innovation. As such, he or she still needs to understand all the details surrounding it. After gaining knowledge about the innovation, the subject will shape his or her attitude, meaning that the persuasion stage follows the knowledge stage in the innovation-decision process.

The knowledge stage is more cognitive (or knowledge) centered, while the persuasion stage is more affective (or feeling) centered, making the individual more sensitively involved with the innovation. However, social reinforcement from others (colleagues, peers, etc.) affect an individual's opinions and beliefs about innovation. Close peers' subjective appraisals of the innovation lessen uncertainties surrounding innovation outcomes and are usually deemed more credible.

At the *decision* stage of the innovation-decision process, an individual must decide whether to adopt or reject the innovation. If the innovation has a partial trial basis, the adoption process is usually accelerated, as individuals prefer to initially try it in their own situation before making an adoption decision. Notwithstanding, rejection is plausible across all stages of the innovation-decision process. Two main types of rejection have been identified: active rejection and passive rejection. In active rejection, the individual tries an innovation, contemplates adopting it, but ultimately decides against it. The most common example of this situation is technological discontinuance. For passive rejection (or non-adoption), the person does not even contemplate adoption.

At the implementation stage, an innovation is put into action. During this phase, the innovation is put to use by the adopter, thanks to information at disposition and technical support. Reinvention generally occurs at this stage, defined as "the degree to which an innovation is changed or modified by a user in the process of its adoption and implementation" (Rogers, 2003, p. 180). The more reinvention takes place, the faster an innovation is adopted and institutionalized.

Finally, the last phase pertains to the *confirmation*. During the confirmation stage, the subject looks for reinforcement for their choice. In this phase, thanks to user experiences and feedback, the subject decides whether or not to continue to use the innovation. Discontinuance can still happen in two ways. The first revolves around whether or not the individual rejects the innovation in order to adopt a better one. This is known as replacement discontinuance. The other type is called disenchantment discontinuance, and this is when the individual does not find the innovation satisfactory in performance or it does not meet their needs.

Communication Channels

Rogers (2003) defines communication has a process through which people create and share information in order to reach mutual comprehension. This communication occurs through channels between sources, which are represented by an individual or institution creating a message, and the recipients (Turnbull & Meenaghan, 1980). There are two types of communication channels: mass media and interpersonal communication. Mass media channels include a mass medium. Instead, interpersonal paths involve two-way communication between two or more persons. Rogers also notes that the diffusion of innovation relies on interpersonal communication. The diffusion of innovation is, in fact, a social process that involves interpersonal communication and relationships occurring between two individuals either within or outside of an organization. In this regard, interpersonal channels are more powerful in creating or changing strong attitudes than mass media channels (Nilakanta & Scamell, 1990).

Hereby, the theory postulates that innovation diffuses through communication, as it allows other people to become more aware of the innovative traits of a technology.

Time

Temporal elements are frequently disregarded in most innovation studies. Yet, according to Rogers, the time aspect in diffusion research is fundamental. The innovation-diffusion process adopter categorization is based on a temporal element (Ghoshal & Bartlett, 1988). Time is fundamental, and many innovations have failed because they were too far ahead in terms of the time of their application in the real world.

Social System

The social system is the final element characterizing the diffusion process. It has been defined as the network of relationships between related individuals, all of whom are involved in a common issue regarding innovation and are seeking to attain a shared objective (Robertson, 1967). Because the diffusion of the innovation locus is the social system, it is also influenced by the social construction of the first. Structure relates to the organized plans of the individuals in a framework, and the idea of the social system influences individuals' inventiveness and their attitudes toward technology (Cool et al., 1997).

Social systems are frequently neglected in scholarly literature and research. However, this research could change perspectives on technology diffusion. Further discussion will be provided in successive sections (Sáenz-Royo et al., 2015).

4.1.1   Obtaining Competitive Advantages Through Technological Innovation

Technological innovation adoption can influence a company's competitive advantage. Thanks to new technology, a company could increase its efficiency and its market reach through innovative production or communication solutions. In this regard, it is fundamental that we understand the dynamics that are capable of fostering such a phenomenon.

According to Rogers (2003), technological innovation can generate a competitive advantage, whether users decide to adopt it on the basis of compatibility, trialability, observability, or its potential to deconstruct complexity.

Compatibility is the extent to which an innovation is perceived as compatible with the existing values, prior experiences, and needs of potential adopters. Poor compatibility with individual needs may have an adverse impact on an individual's technology usage. When a technology is compatible with an individual's needs, then the level of uncertainty will be reduced and the rate of adoption of the innovation will be accelerated. Likewise, a new technology also needs to be compatible with existing legacy infrastructure and architecture. On the one hand, the use is motivated by compatibility with individual skills (Vukomanovic et al., 2016). On the other hand, adoption may be fostered by the fact that it is compatible with other tools and, thus, is perceived to be easier to use.

The importance of *trialability* is highlighted through certain elements of the innovation-decision process. Trialability can thus be defined as the extent to which an innovation can be experimented with on a limited basis. Trialability is correlated with the rate of adoption: the more an innovation is tried, the more quickly it is adopted. In addition, during the trial stage of the innovation-decision process, potential adopters can modify or alter the innovation. This is a phenomenon known as reinvention, and it can expedite the adoption process. Lastly, vicarious trials are especially important for later adopters and can increase the adoption rate of an innovation (Laurell et al., 2019). However, research has shown that the trialability attribute of innovations is more important for early adopters (those not reliant on peer feedback) than for later adopters.

Observability is then the extent to which the effects of an invention are observable by others. Role modeling (or peer observation) is an essential element fostering the acceptance of technology. Observability is associated with a higher rate of adoption, consist with compatibility and trialability (Labay & Kinnear, 1981).

Finally, the *possibility to deconstruct complexity* is the degree to which an innovation is perceived as difficult but understandable in its usage. Excessive complexity is an obstacle to adoption. On the other hand, if a technology is user-friendly, then it might be adopted more successfully (Chen & Kamal, 2016).

In conclusion, innovations with greater advantages should possess the qualities of compatibility, simplicity, trialability, and observability in order to be adopted more rapidly than other innovations. Although introducing and gaining acceptance of a new idea can be a challenge, the aforementioned characteristics will expedite the process of innovation diffusion.

4.2   A Role for Relational Goods in Diffusion of Innovation

As we begin to acknowledge the importance of new technologies within businesses, one thing that has been deemed fundamental is the observation of the social factors that might trigger the willingness of the workforce to adopt them (Fromm, 2023). Although it has been included in the diffusion of innovation framework since its development, one of the most neglected factors is the social system.

Diffusion of Innovation, indeed, originates as a sociological framework that seeks to explain how, why, and at what rate new ideas, practices, and technologies spread through a social system. Hence, the social system needs to play a major role in influencing the spread of innovation.

Social networks are a key factor in the diffusion of innovation. These networks create pathways for the spread of information and ideas and facilitate the adoption of new practices and technologies. While individuals may be aware of an innovation, they are more likely to adopt it if they have access to someone in their social network who is already using it (Fromm, 2023). Social network members can share their experiences and knowledge with each other, which can further encourage the adoption of an innovation (Tavares et al., 2022).

With this in mind, the structure of a social system affects the rate of diffusion of innovation. Structural factors, such as the size and composition of the population, the availability of resources, and the presence of shared values and norms, all shape the diffusion process (Pirson et al., 2019). Similarly, shared values and norms can influence individuals to adopt an innovation more readily (Melè, 2016).

While the association of relational goods within the company have already found relevance in technology-related decisions, in the context of diffusion of innovation, they are yet to be conceptualized. However, building on these premises, the importance of relational goods can be assessed.

As relational goods are based on interpersonal relationships and mutual recognition within a work context, these goods could potentially fit within the social system component of innovation diffusion (Singh & Babbar, 2021). Specifically, they could represent the underlying structure of the values, norms, and relationships that shape how a social context is articulated (Koon, 2021). Companies with high levels of relational goods could potentially benefit from a well-structured internal network in which employees seek to collaborate to tackle common problems (Roszkowska & Melè, 2021). Likewise, in these contexts, empathy between employees could allow staff to be more willing to share information with each other and help colleagues in need (Koon, 2021).

With this in mind, relational goods represent an element characterizing the social system within the Diffusion of Innovation Theory.

The research section of this book will observe how relational goods can affect the digital transformation of a company.

References

Chen, W., & Kamal, F. (2016). The impact of information and communication technology adoption on multinational firm boundary decisions. *Journal of International Business Studies, 47*, 563–576.

Cool, K. O., Dierickx, I., & Szulanski, G. (1997). Diffusion of innovations within organizations: Electronic switching in the Bell system, 1971–1982. *Organization Science, 8*(5), 543–559.

Elmghaamez, I. K., Attah-Boakye, R., Adams, K., & Agyemang, J. (2022). The diffusion of innovation theory and the effects of IFRS adoption by multinational corporations on capital market performance: A cross-country analysis. *Thunderbird International Business Review, 64*(1), 81–108.

English, P. (2016). Twitter's diffusion in sports journalism: Role models, laggards and followers of the social media innovation. *New Media & Society, 18*(3), 484–501.

Fromm, E. (2023). *The revolution of hope: Toward a humanized technology.* Open Road Media.

Ghoshal, S., & Bartlett, C. A. (1988). Creation, adoption and diffusion of innovations by subsidiaries of multinational corporations. *Journal of International Business Studies, 19*, 365–388.

Koon, V. Y. (2021). Bibliometric analyses on the emergence and present growth of humanistic management. *International Journal of Ethics and Systems, 37*(4), 581–598.

Labay, D. G., & Kinnear, T. C. (1981). Exploring the consumer decision process in the adoption of solar energy systems. *Journal of Consumer Research, 8*(3), 271–278.

Laurell, C., Sandström, C., Berthold, A., & Larsson, D. (2019). Exploring barriers to adoption of Virtual Reality through Social Media Analytics and Machine Learning–An assessment of technology, network, price and trialability. *Journal of Business Research, 100*, 469–474.

Lundblad, J. P. (2003). A review and critique of Rogers' diffusion of innovation theory as it applies to organizations. *Organization Development Journal, 21*(4), 50–60.

Melé, D. (2016). Understanding humanistic management. *Humanistic Management Journal, 1*, 33–55.

Nilakanta, S., & Scamell, R. W. (1990). The effect of information sources and communication channels on the diffusion of innovation in a data base development environment. *Management Science, 36*(1), 24–40.

Pirson, M., Vázquez-Maguirre, M., Corus, C., Steckler, E., & Wicks, A. (2019). Dignity and the process of social innovation: Lessons from social entrepreneurship and transformative services for humanistic management. *Humanistic Management Journal, 4*, 125–153.

Robertson, T. S. (1967). The process of innovation and the diffusion of innovation. *Journal of Marketing, 31*(1), 14–19.

Rogers, E. M. (2003). *Diffusion of innovations* (5th ed.). Free Press.

Roszkowska, P., & Melé, D. (2021). Organizational factors in the individual ethical behaviour. The notion of the "organizational moral structure". *Humanistic Management Journal, 6*, 187–209.

Sáenz-Royo, C., Gracia-Lázaro, C., & Moreno, Y. (2015). The role of the organization structure in the diffusion of innovations. *PLoS One, 10*(5), e0126076.

Singh, R. K., & Babbar, M. (2021). Religious Diversity at Workplace: A Literature Review. *Humanistic Management Journal, 6*, 229–247.

Tavares, M. C., Azevedo, G., & Marques, R. P. (2022). The Challenges and Opportunities of Era 5.0 for a More Humanistic and Sustainable Society—A Literature Review. *Societies, 12*(6), 149–170.

Turnbull, P. W., & Meenaghan, A. (1980). Diffusion of innovation and opinion leadership. *European Journal of Marketing, 14*(1), 3–33.

Valente, T. W. (1996). Social network thresholds in the diffusion of innovations. *Social Networks, 18*(1), 69–89.

Vukomanovic, M., Young, M., & Huynink, S. (2016). IPMA ICB 4.0—A global standard for project, programme and portfolio management competences. *International Journal of Project Management, 34*(8), 1703–1705.

Zenko, Z., & Mulej, M. (2011). Diffusion of innovative behaviour with social responsibility. *Kybernetes, 40*(9/10), 1258–1272.

Zhou, Y. (2008). Voluntary adopters versus forced adopters: Integrating the diffusion of innovation theory and the technology acceptance model to study intra-organizational adoption. *New Media & Society, 10*(3), 475–496.

Zhu, Q., Sarkis, J., & Lai, K. H. (2012). Green supply chain management innovation diffusion and its relationship to organizational improvement: An ecological modernization perspective. *Journal of Engineering and Technology Management, 29*(1), 168–185.

CHAPTER 5

Empirical Observation of the Importance of Relational Goods in SMEs

Abstract Building on Diffusion of Innovation (DOI) Theory and relational goods, real-world business cases have been explored. In particular, the analysis has been conducted through the use of a mixed-method analysis. Firstly, managers of the companies were interviewed to investigate how they nurture relationship within their respective organizations. Second, a survey has been administered to employees. Results show how relational goods fit within the DOI Theory and could help a smooth digital transformation process in SMEs.

Keywords Digital transformation management • Case study • Structural equation modeling • Mixed-method analysis • Humanistic management • Digital strategies

5.1 ANALYTICAL APPROACH

The objective of this manuscript is twofold. First, the authors wished to explore the importance of humanistic management in SMEs. Second, an analysis on the importance of relational goods in digital transformation projects wished to be performed.

Two research questions may then be proposed:

© The Author(s), under exclusive license to Springer Nature Switzerland AG 2023
A. Marrucci, R. Rialti, *Successful Digital Transformation Initiatives in SMEs*, https://doi.org/10.1007/978-3-031-36465-5_5

RQ1: *Is humanistic management a relevant approach for SMEs, and if so, which are the actions managers could perform to implement it?*
RQ2: *Which is the role of relational goods in digital transformation projects?*

To attempt to reply these two research questions, a mixed-method study has been performed. First, a series of interviews with SMEs managers have been conducted. In total five semi-structured interviews have been performed with three managers of three SMEs belonging to the same owners. Second, a conceptual model has been developed and tested through structural equation modeling (SEM). Data were obtained through 301 surveys administered to employees of the previously indicated businesses.

We deemed this approach suitable as it was necessary to explain how the theoretical idea could be corroborated with real-world findings.

In particular, the qualitative part of the research allowed the authors to determine the importance of humanistic management in SMEs and to develop a set of guidelines for managers wishing to apply it in their businesses (Acevedo, 2012). Then, the quantitative approach allowed to observe the importance of relational goods for employees involved in organizational change processes. In particular, it allowed to unpack how a humanistic strategy (namely, the development of relational goods) applied in businesses may change internal communication structures, thus fostering employees' acceptance of new technologies (Zald, 1993).

5.2   Selected Cases

Alpha, Beta, and Gamma are three SMEs from Tuscany (Italy). They are owned by the same family, which is engaged directly in the operations. Yet, the three companies, in spite of their size, are also characterized by a coordinated managerial structure with a general director in each one and several line managers. Each of the company has about 100–150 employees. Among their principal processes, it is possible to cite galvanic, Physical Vapor Deposition (PVD), cataphoretic, and regular varnishing, etc. In such a regard, they operate in fashion accessories industry.

The principal strategic goal of this group of businesses concerns the conclusion of a multi-step digital transformation process that initiated four years ago.

The cases have been deemed appropriate for two reasons. First of all, while the three SMEs operate autonomously, they belong to the same owners. Hence, global strategies such as technology strategy and HRM strategy are common for all the three companies as they were one. Second, as each company is working autonomously, the selection allowed to reach a number of respondents exposed to common policies suitable for the investigation in SMEs context.

In addition, top management and some of the owners defined themselves as "humanists borrowed to management." Consistently, they have focused on creating policies in all companies to engage employees through community building (Pirson & Lawrence, 2010). As relational goods are strictly related to relationships arousing from communities existing within a business, the authors deemed it as relevant to evaluate the impact of these intangible goods.

5.3   PRELIMINARY QUALITATIVE OBSERVATION

To investigate the importance of humanism in SMEs management, three managers of the companies were interviewed (two of them were interviewed twice). In particular, semi-structured interviews were selected as the main instrument for data collection.

Starting protocol concerned three main topics: (1) why humanistic management were selected; (2) which humanism principles were applied; (3) how humanistic management principles were deployed in practice.

Responses were transcript. A corpus of about 20 pages of text in Italian was developed. It corresponded to about six hours of interviews. This text then was printed and analyzed by the authors to identify the main codes shared by all the responses.

The principal results are the following ones.

Identification of Humanistic Management as a Suitable Approach to Management
Two of the interviewed managers shared a common humanistic background. In particular, one got a master's degree in modern language, the other one in philosophy (Zald, 1993). They shared a similar background in term of previous work positions, as both were marketing managers promoted to general managers.

For them, the integration of humanism principles in management was something quite natural. The third one was instead impressed by the climate in other SMEs and decided to start to get documented on how certain results were obtained (Aktouf, 1992).

Building on the premises, all the three companies started to adopt similar strategies.

The main reason of the selection of humanism-bound approaches may be summarized by this quote from the general manager of Gamma:

Businesses are communities, the more people feel themselves as a part of something bigger than their own self, the more they will start to behave to pursue a common goal which may generate mutual benefits.

Selected Humanistic Principles

The first act performed by each of the three managers was the identification of the humanism principles most suitable for their cases (Acevedo, 2012).

In such a regard, all the three of them agreed on the importance of dignity and equality in the workplace as the first two principles to be transmitted to employees (Pirson, 2017). These two principles provided normative rules for employees; they started to act as a respectful group of colleagues, aiming for the same objective and accepting the opinion of everyone else within the business.

Then, they stressed the importance of critical thinking. In such a regard, the three managers jointly developed mechanisms to incentive employees to communicate with them and with their supervisors, mostly by providing feedbacks even in the case these ones were unfavorable in respect of managerial actions. The development of critical thinking showed employees management's openness and tolerance, which allowed for the development of mutual trust (Pirson & Lawrence, 2010).

Such an occurrence is stressed also by the words of the manager from Alpha:

I found in need to change the way I was dealing with the employees of Alpha. To complete the transformation, I was desperate about getting their feedbacks. I got almost immediately how the best way to convince them to provide feedbacks was to show openness and tolerance in respect of their opinions. It took long time, but I was capable to obtain their trust. Now were treat each other as peers.

In the moment the manager/employee barrier started to break, even the relationship between employees started to change. The most interesting result was that employees started to talk in first-person plural and not in first-person singular. Managers identified this moment as a turning point. From that moment they identified the birth of communities within the business, which later on developed as a complete business community encompassing almost everyone in the plant (Chan et al., 2018).

In such a regard, the general manager of Beta stressed:

> *I felt the success of the initiative when I observed senior employees extremely convinced about the need to include younger ones in different activities. Likewise, I was surprised by the number of interesting questions older employees started to ask about digital technologies.*

Deployment of Humanistic Principles
All the three managers agreed on the importance for managers to set the example. In particular, they observed the need to start to behave differently with employees (Koon, 2021).

In the moment the relationship between managers and employees started to change, they developed training courses focused on the importance of interpersonal relationship in the company (Melé, 2016).

Information about the ways to deploy humanistic principles in SMEs are provided in this chapter.

5.4 Structural Equation Modeling

5.4.1 Conceptual Model and Research Instrument

Building on the DOI theoretical framework, we developed a conceptual model structured around two independent and three dependent variables. Central to this model is the notion of innovation, defined as "an idea, practice, or project considered new by an individual or other adopting unit" (Rogers, 2003, p. 12). To ensure innovation acceptance, employees must associate this novelty with a perceived benefit. Relative advantage is defined as the degree to which an innovation is seen as better than its predecessor (Choudhury & Karahanna, 2008). Therefore, we posit that to facilitate digital transformation within a company, employees must perceive the use of new technologies as more efficient than the old ones. To explore this construct of relative advantage, we used the scale validated by Erskine et al. (2019), which seeks to measure employees' perceptions of the new technology-work task efficiency relationship. The second element of the diffusion of innovation is communication channels. For Rogers (2003), communication is a process in which participants create and share information with each other to achieve mutual understanding. Moreover, "diffusion is a very social process involving interpersonal communication relationships" (Rogers, 2003, p. 19). Interpersonal channels are more powerful in creating or changing an individual's strong attitudes. In interpersonal channels, communication may have a characteristic of homogeneity, which is "the degree to which two or more interacting individuals are similar in some attributes, such as beliefs, education, socioeconomic status, and the like," but the diffusion of innovations requires at least some degree of heterogeneity, which is "the degree to which two or more interacting individuals are different in some attributes" (Rogers, 2003, p. 19). Based on these considerations, the present research assumes that relational goods may express the concept of appropriate communicative channel for technological diffusion. In fact, relational goods are non-instrumental social relationships based on trust and shared learning and derive from interpersonal and reflexive elements. As outlined by Rogers (2003), intersubjectivity is the essential prerequisite for developing appropriate communicative channels. This aspect is central to the construct of relational goods, as developing stable relationships requires the encounter between two or more people (Donati, 2019). The encounter itself promotes communication between employees. In addition, Rogers (2003) clarifies how in interpersonal communication channels, a necessary aspect that enables the diffusion of technological innovations lies in heterogeneity. In fact, while individuals with the same characteristics and beliefs may perceive an innovation as good and accept it, companies are made up of heterogeneous people in whom personal and social attributes and characteristics differ. The challenge then lies in the fact that only when the total ity of diverse people has understood and accepted the need for change, high degrees of digital transformation can be achieved. Since relational goods are composed of a reflexive element (Donati, 2019), we believe that through reflexivity it is possible to synthesize multiplicity into a kind of oneness. By reflecting on the other person's position and point of view, and accepting diversity, it is possible to transform heterogeneity into homogeneity. When relationships are structured around intersubjective and reflexive aspects, the relationship itself is able to promote benefits, that is, intangible elements that stand between people (Donati & Solci, 2011). These intangible relational goods can refer to trust and the development of an excellent collaborative climate within the company; both aspects will foster processes of technological diffusion. We assume that relational goods, that is, intersubjective and reflexive social relations, are appropriate communication channels to foster the promotion, diffusion, and acceptance of technological transformations, as through these human relations an individual seeks to understand the other's point of view while trying to explain why certain changes are necessary. Solci (2009) identified 30 structural and attitude indicators through which the two dimensions that compose relational goods can be conceptualized. Regarding intersubjective relationship, the first indicator refers to the time that is spent on activities that presuppose being with others. Time is a scarce resource that deserves to be investigated in order to understand how a person decides to allocate it. The second indicator emphasizes the monetary investments that a person allocates in activities without intersubjective relationships, while the increase in new knowledge represents the third index. The assumption here holds that if an individual manifests a willingness to expand the number of relationships and knowledge, then he or she will increase his or her propensity to produce relational goods. Resilience is able to transform vicious intersubjective relationships into virtuous ones while supportiveness is understood as a circumstance of full reciprocity. If an action is supportive, it will be a producer of relational goods. The sixth indicator is companionship: meeting with other people, as opposed to autonomy or isolation, can foster the development of relational goods. Sociability, empathy, and solidarity are values that lead individuals to produce relational goods. Another indicator is reciprocity, a central aspect of social relations. Thus follow, four indicators on the values attributed to intersubjective relationships: loyalty to the relationship, gratitude, tolerance, and transcendence of the relationship (Solci, 2009).

Each of these 14 indicators has been associated with respective items that can clarify the intersubjective component of relational goods.

The reflective component is explained by Solci (2009) through the use of 16 indicators.

The first four indicators refer to the instrumental component of the social relationship: prejudice, communication skills, adaptation, and understanding of positions different from one's own. The author also explores other set of indicators such as gratification and helping, which represent fundamental component of social behavior. Other indices include value aspects like relational intensity, informality, and habit, which is considered a relational element since the value of a good would emerge stably when it is not experienced as a routine.

Based on these indicators, 16 items expressing the reflexive relationship were developed. Besides having been used by sociologists Donati and

Solci (2011) in the sociological field, this scale was also applied in a study by Marrucci et al. (2020, 2022), linking it to aspects such as commitment and turnover. The presence of intersubjective and reflexive relationships has been shown to promote the emergence of relational goods, that is, intangible benefits that have the ability to reduce employees' willingness to leave the organization. It is necessary to emphasize that although relational goods are those intangible benefits derived from intersubjective and reflexive relationships, their measurement must necessarily focus on the individual, and in agreement with Solci (2009), we assume that depending on the importance and attitude a person associates with intersubjective and reflexive relationships, high or low degrees of relational goods may emerge.

Moreover, relational goods are generative elements, in that sociality, relationality, and understanding of others can give rise to positive changes that regenerate a system. The social system is the last element in the diffusion process. Rogers (2003) defined the social system as "a set of interrelated units engaged in joint problem solving to achieve a common goal" (p. 23). As the diffusion of innovations occurs in the social system, it is affected by the social structure within the system. When a firm values and cares for the intersubjective and reflexive relationships that may emerge among its employees, this same valuing represents the structure of the social system. For these reasons, relational goods, that is, intersubjective and reflexive relationships, are considered both as an appropriate communication channel for the diffusion of technological innovations and as the backbone of the social system. While both perceived relative advantages and relational goods can foster processes of technological transformation and diffusion, these two relationships could be mediated by other constructs. In fact, we assume that an appropriate interpersonal and reflective communication channel can foster technological transformation of a company only if the key players in the relationship also perceive support from the manager (Bouckenooghe et al., 2009). In this sense, early formulations of the concept of change readiness identified "principal support" as a key factor in employee change readiness (Armenakis & Bedeian, 1999). On a daily basis, management support helps employees cope with the demands of their role (Bakker et al., 2004), with clearly positive effects on organizational outcomes, such as employee engagement, motivation, and well-being. These effects persist in the context of organizational change, such that supportive relationships lead to more positive employee attitudes toward change (Jimmieson et al., 2009). On the one hand, relationality is a suitable communication channel for the diffusion of technological change; on the other hand, it may be necessary for employees to perceive their manager's support in change processes. We assume that relationality could also positively foster employees' perceptions toward support, as relational goods are structured on understanding and openness toward others, qualifying as an additional positive, interpersonal communication channel with their managers. Moreover, the positive perception that employees might have about a technology (perceived relative advantage) could also increase the need for perceived management support. To analyze the construct perceived management support, we used the scale of Bouckenooghe et al. (2009). Another mediating variable lies in information sharing (adapted from Youndt et al., 2004). Youndt et al. (2004) developed a set of items to capture the extent to which organizational stakeholders exchange and share information and knowledge. We adapted their measure to reflect the ways in which the employee exchanges and shares information with colleagues. In our model, this latent variable is positively related to relational goods and perceived relative advantage. We hypothesize that high levels of relational goods may promote information exchange among employees, as these types of relationships are based on mutual help and mutual understanding. Furthermore, we hypothesize that when employees perceive a new technology positively because it can provide work benefits, this same perception can promote their willingness to collaborate with others and exchange information.

Finally, the conceptual model presents an outcome variable defined as digital transformation (Nasiri et al., 2020). In this study, we describe this variable as the transformation of the firm at process, culture, and organizational levels to meet the needs of the market through digital technologies. Digital transformation involves rethinking, reimagining, and redesigning the company in the digital age (Hinings et al., 2018). We hypothesize that the diffusion of this new digital vision may occur as a result of the variables we described above; therefore, relative advantage, relational goods, perceived management support, and information exchange could all positively influence digital transformation.

Please see below the detail of the selected constructs used in the analysis (Fig. 5.1).

Selected Constructs Composing the Administered Survey
(A) Perceived Relative Advantage

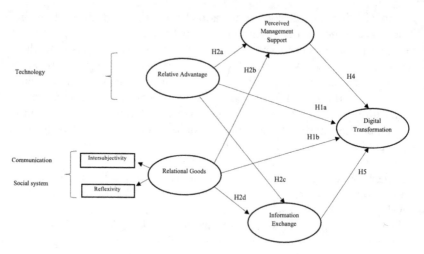

Fig. 5.1   Conceptual model

Erskine, M. A., Khojah, M., & McDaniel, A. E. (2019). Location selection using heat maps: Relative advantage, task-technology fit, and decision-making performance. *Computers in Human Behavior, 101,* 151–162.

RA1—Using (technology) enables me to accomplish tasks more quickly.
RA2—Using (technology) improves the quality of tasks I do.
RA3—Using (technology) makes it easier to do tasks.
RA4—Using (technology) enhances my effectiveness of my tasks.
RA5—Using (technology) increases my productivity.

(B) Relational Goods
Donati, P., & Solci, R. (2011). *I beni relazionali. Che cosa sono e quali effetti producono.* Milano: FrancoAngeli. Translated.

Intersubjective Relationship

IR1—I spend time on activities with intersubjective relationships.
IR2—I prefer to spend on dining or traveling with friends than to buying a state-of-the-art television set.
IR3—It is better to make new friends than to hang out with the usual people.

IR4—To overcome disagreements, dialogue must be re-established first.
IR5—Being together with others relieves tensions.
IR6—Being alone is sad.
IR7—Having lunch together with colleagues is a pleasant habit.
IR8—It is useful talking to someone to understand our mistakes.
IR9—Taking yourself seriously requires confidence.
IR10—When an opportunity arises, others won't screw us over.
IR11—People's needs have the same relevance as ours.
IR12—Gratitude is demonstrated in person, with daily gestures.
IR13—If a friend treats me rudely, I should continue to see him or her.
IR14—There is only one human nature, different purposes and expressions are expressions of similar desires.

Reflexive Relationship

RR1—To avoid risks, it is better to relate to people who look good.
RR2—People often understand our moods and feelings.
RR3—It's good to meet people you've lost touch with.
RR4—It is useful to discuss with people who have different opinions from ours.
RR5—Being with friends makes you feel good about yourself.
RR6—When you have problems, you can always count on the help of others.
RR7—Conversation is a pleasant way to spend time.
RR8—Money matters do not threaten a fraternal friendship.
RR9—Establishing a reputation helps to build stable relationships.
RR10—It is important to have a close and informal relationship with friends.
RR11—It is important to meet friends even if you don't want to, otherwise you might lose them.
RR12—Giving confidence rarely leads to disappointment.
RR13—It is always possible to find common ground with people who think differently.
RR14—Love requires reciprocity.
RR15—Friendships depend more on our will than on habits.
RR16—Meditating in solitude makes us understand the meaning of life.

(C) Perceived Management Support
Bouckenooghe, D., Devos, G., & Van den Broeck, H. (2009). Organizational change questionnaire–climate of change, processes, and readiness: Development of a new instrument. *The Journal of psychology, 143*(6), 559–599.

PMS1—Our department's senior managers pay sufficient attention to the personal consequences that the changes could have for their staff members.

PMS2—Our department's senior managers coach us very well about implementing change.

PMS3—Our department's senior managers have trouble in adapting their leadership styles to the changes.

PMS4—My manager does not seem very keen to help me find a solution if I have a problem.

PMS5—If I experience any problems, I can always turn on my manager for help.

PMS6—My manager can place herself/himself in my position.

PMS7—My manager encourages me to do things that I have never done before.

(D) Information Exchange
Youndt, M. A., Subramaniam M., & Snell S. A. (2004). Intellectual capital profiles: An examination of investments and returns. *Journal of Management Studies, 41*(2), 335–361.

IE1—I like to collaborate with other employees to solve problems.

IE2—It is important to share information at work, learning from others.

IE3—I interact and exchange ideas with people working in different areas of the organization.

IE4—I apply the knowledge I have learned to solve problems.

(E) Digital Transformation
Nasiri, M., Ukko, J., Saunila, M., & Rantala, T. (2020). Managing the digital supply chain: The role of smart technologies. *Technovation, 96*, 102121.

DT1—In the business I work for, we will digitalize everything that can be digitalized.

DT2—In the business I work for, we collect large amounts of data from different sources.

DT3—In the business I work for, we aim to create stronger networking between the different business processes with digital technologies.

DT4—In the business I work for, we aim to enhance an efficient customer interface with digitality.

DT5—In the business I work for, we aim at achieving information exchange with digitality.

5.4.2   Hypotheses

According to the Diffusion of Innovation Theory, we assume:

H1a: Perceived technology Relative advantage may promote Digital Transformation.

H1b: Relational Goods may create a proper communication arena able to promote Digital Transformation.

The two independent variables may positively influence:

H2a: Perceived technology Relative advantage may positively affect Perceived Management Support.

H2b: Relational Goods, which are part of the social system of the business, may positively influence Perceived Management Support.

H2c: Perceived technology Relative advantage may positively influence Information Exchange.

H2d Relational Goods may foster Information Exchange.

Further:

H4: Perceived Management support may positively influence Digital Transformation.

H5: Information Sharing may positively influence Digital Transformation.

5.4.3   Data Collection

To empirically test the hypothesized relationships, we decide to use a sample of Italian SMEs working in manufacturing companies in the galvanic sector, which is an industry that has had to undertake major Industry 4.0

technology investments. The target group is employees, and the question-naires were completed on site. We were able to collect 301 responses, divided into 53% men and 47% women with an age range of 31–45 years for 47%. The sample size was adequate to conduct structural equation modelling analyses (Kline, 2015). We conducted statistical analysis through the use of SPSS which has provided the conditions to extract some considerations in terms of reliability and variance referred to the dimensions of relational goods. According to the traditional two-step analysis of covariance-based structural equation modeling (CB-SEM), was performed a measurement model assessed the psychometric properties of the hypothesized model constructs; next, a structural model examined the statistical influences between the latent variables.

5.4.4   Results

The following pages will report the results of our empirical analysis. The first section is dedicated to statistical results, while the second section will report the findings of structural equation analysis.

5.4.4.1   Statistical Results and Correlation Analysis

We proceeded to calculate the reliability of each construct and their cor-relations. Adequacy is evaluated using Cronbach's Alpha coefficient. This measurement verifies the effectiveness of the scales examined. Values below the critical limit (0.60) must necessarily be discarded. Relative advantage achieves a high level of reliability (0.940). Since relational goods is a second-degree variable, we calculated the reliability of the two ele-ments that compose the construct: intersubjective relationship (0.730) and reflexive relationship (0.854). Perceived management support's items show not very high values but still above the threshold level (0.645). Information exchange is the second mediator of our conceptual model, composed by four items and its Cronbach's Alpha is 0.837. Digital trans-formation, which is our last dependent variable, shows very high reliability with values above 0.9 (0.910). Once analyzed the different inter-item cor-relations that judge or prejudice the reliability of the single latent vari-ables, it is useful to observe what degree of correlation there is between them. Through Pearson's correlation index we have analyzed the systemic relationship between the model variables. Intersubjective relationship and reflexive relationship are the most positively correlated variables. This result is indispensable because, as widely discussed in the previous pages, it would be the union of the two relations to give origin to the construct of relational goods ($r = 0.805$). Following this perspective, it is possible to explain the notion of social relation, moving away from the economic conceptualizations of relation and clinging to the sociological sphere. These types of relationships also exhibit optimal values with respect to perceived management support, information exchange, and digital transformation. In particular, the two constructs are correlated with the mediating and dependent variables for higher values than the independent variable relative advantage. These results may anticipate that non-instrumental social relationships based on mutual help and shared growth may be a valuable communicative and social channel for promoting benefits that result, for example, in technological diffusion and organizational change. Relationality would also seem to be the key element compared to the perceived benefits of using a new technology.

Table 5.1 shows the statistical results obtained.

5.4.4.2 Structural Model and Results

Finally, to test our assumptions, we evaluated statistical influences among latent variables, through the use of covariance-based structural equation modeling (CB-SEM).

We first tested whether the relative advantage that employees associate with using a new technology could promote high degrees of digital transformation. In particular, we wish to verify if H1a is supported and if the first element of technology diffusion has an impact in promoting technological change. As demonstrated in Fig. 5.2 the H1a is supported as $\beta = +0.433$; $p<0.01$.

Table 5.1 Statistical results

Variables	1	2	3	4	5	6
1. Relative Advantage	1.000					
2. Intersubjective Relationship	0.191**	1.000				
3. Reflexive Relationship	0.140*	0.805**	1.000			
4. Perceived Management Support	0.335**	0.517**	0.430**	1.000		
5. Information Exchange	0.285**	0.507**	0.578**	0.366**	1.000	
6. Digital Transformation	0.435**	0.491**	0.465**	0.473**	0.649**	1.000
Mean	6.017	4.517	4.700	4.451	5.583	5.092
Cronbach's Alpha	0.940	0.730	0.854	0.645	0.837	0.910

Fig. 5.2 H1a

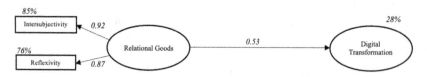

Fig. 5.3 H1b

Then, we examined if relational goods could be qualified as an appropriate communicative channel for the diffusion of technological changes. The results in Fig. 5.3 show that relational goods not only consist of intersubjective and reflexive elements but also have a positive impact on technology diffusion and digital changes (β = +0.533; $p<0.01$). Thus, it has been demonstrated that communication and social channels are key elements of technology diffusion compared to the perception of relative advantages. Non-instrumental relationships based on mutual support can promote change and progress. H1a and H1b have been proven.

Then, we hypothesized that perceived management support and information exchange could qualify as mediating variables of the two main relationships analyzed. Figure 5.4 shows the results obtained.

As shown in Fig. 5.4, all our hypotheses have been proven. Indeed, both perceived relative advantages and relational goods have a positive impact on perceived management support (H2a: β = +0.165; $p<0.01$; H2b: β = +0.534; $p<0.01$) and information sharing (H2c: β = +0.181; $p<0.01$; H2d: β = +0.581; $p<0.01$). However, it is necessary to emphasize how relational goods exert a greater weight on the two mediating variables, reinforcing the idea that in the diffusion of new technological paradigms, the presence of communicative channels based on mutual learning favors (1) the exchange of information, (2) the relationship between employees and management, and (3) the digital transformation of the company. Following this perspective, it can further be seen that information exchange has a higher positive effect on digital transformation than

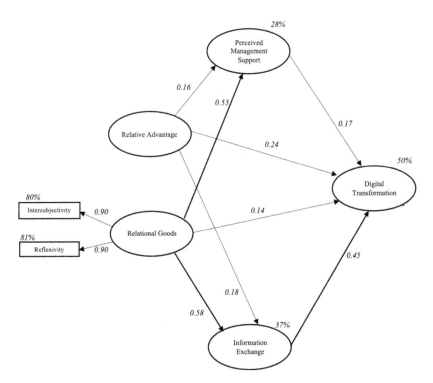

Fig. 5.4 Overall results of conceptual model

management support. This result strengthens the idea that relationships are at the basis of any type of change.

5.5 Overall Results

The purpose of this book was to understand the role of non-instrumental relations in the processes of technology diffusion. Specifically, we used the sociological construct of relational goods to conceptualize a new type of social relations that are structured around the concepts of intersubjectivity and reflexivity (Donati, 2019). In fact, relationships presuppose encounters from multiple actors and recognition of others' diversity. Therefore, only when one seeks to understand the point of view of others and reflects on differences is it possible to provide an opening for social relationships that lead to personal and social growth (Gui, 1987). These kinds of relationships give rise to intangible realities that can be classified as relational goods. Relational goods are thus social relations in which people grow and learn from each other. We have shown that in the processes of technological diffusion, these types of social relations can qualify as a valuable communicative tool capable of diffusing and promoting change. We assume that in the presence of relational goods, it is possible to embrace change without losing one's personal and social identity and thus finding new meaning at work. Relational goods can increase the creation of meaning and reducing the isolation that employees may feel in the face of technological change. As expected, we were able to confirm the construct of relational goods as a first-order variable composed of two subdimensions, namely, intersubjective and reflexive relationships. In fact, this construct was originally tested primarily in nonprofit organization contexts, so it was not observed how it could be employed as a first-order construct (Donati, 2019; Donati & Solci, 2015). Our results indicate that these two subdimensions are highly associated with the construct of relational goods, which significate that managers of organizations and especially human resource managers should pay attention to these behavioral patterns of employees. Our empirical analysis then showed that relational goods are a significant predictor and antecedent of information exchange and perceived management support, two important key variables according to the organizational change literature (see Marrucci et al., 2020). Relationality can create an ecosystem in which employees truly feel part of a whole. Interestingly, appropriate communication channels have a greater influence on technological diffusion than the perceived benefits obtainable from the new technology. To embrace and support a new technology, employees must perceive that this same technology can improve their current task, yet this perceived benefit has been found to play a secondary role in technology diffusion compared to relationships. Change happens only when communicated and transferred appropriately. Consequently, we suggest that human resource managers invest primarily in the relational assets of the organization (Ahn & Hong, 2019).

Our research, apart from the traditional constraints of survey-based research (i.e., self-reporting), suffers from some limitations. In particular, we focused on only one country, Italy. Also, we did not attempt to develop a new construct of relational good. Third, any antecedents of relational goods have not been explored.

On the basis of the above, we suggest that future researchers re-test our hypothesized model in cultural contexts other than Italy, such as more collectivistic (Asia) or more individualistic (U.S.) countries, to assess whether significant differences occur. In particular, it would be interesting to validate the relational goods construct in other organizational contexts as well and see what kinds of comparisons might emerge from the different statistical influences of the model.

REFERENCES

Acevedo, A. (2012). Personalist business ethics and humanistic management: Insights from Jacques Maritain. *Journal of Business Ethics, 105*, 197–219.

Ahn, J., & Hong, A. J. (2019). Transforming I into we in organizational knowledge creation: A case study. *Human Resource Development Quarterly, 30*(4), 565–582.

Aktouf, O. (1992). Management and theories of organizations in the 1990s: Toward a critical radical humanism? *Academy of Management Review, 17*(3), 407–431.

Armenakis, A. A., & Bedeian, A. G. (1999). Organizational change: A review of theory and research in the 1990s. *Journal of Management, 25*(3), 293–315.

Bakker, A. B., Demerouti, E., & Verbeke, W. (2004). Using the job demands-resources model to predict burnout and performance. *Human Resource Management, 43*(1), 83–104.

Bouckenooghe, D., Devos, G., & Van den Broeck, H. (2009). Organizational change questionnaire–climate of change, processes, and readiness: Development of a new instrument. *The Journal of Psychology, 143*(6), 559–599.

Chan, A. P. C., Darko, A., Olanipekun, A. O., & Ameyaw, E. E. (2018). Critical barriers to green building technologies adoption in developing countries: The case of Ghana. *Journal of Cleaner Production, 172*, 1067–1079.

Choudhury, V., & Karahanna, E. (2008). The relative advantage of electronic channels: A multidimensional view. *MIS Quarterly, 32*, 179–200.

Donati, P. (2019). *Scoprire i beni relazionali. Per generare una nuova socialità.* Rubbettino.

Donati, P., & Solci, R. (2011). *I beni relazionali: che cosa sono e quali effetti producono.* Bollati Boringhieri.

Donati, P., & Solci, R. (2015). Misurare l'immateriale: il caso dei beni relazionali. *Sociologia e Ricerca Sociale, 108*(3), 13–32.

Erskine, M. A., Khojah, M., & McDaniel, A. E. (2019). Location selection using heat maps: Relative advantage, task-technology fit, and decision-making performance. *Computers in Human Behavior, 101*, 151–162.

Gui, B. (1987). Eléments pour une définition d'économie communautaire. *Notes et Documents, 19/20*, 32–42.

Hinings, B., Gegenhuber, T., & Greenwood, R. (2018). Digital innovation and transformation: An institutional perspective. *Information and Organization, 28*(1), 52–61.

Jimmieson, N. L., White, K. M., & Zajdlewicz, L. (2009). Psychosocial predictors of intentions to engage in change supportive behaviors in an organizational context. *Journal of Change Management, 9*(3), 233–250.

Kline, R. B. (2015). *Principles and practice of structural equation modeling*. The Guilford Press.

Koon, V. Y. (2021). Bibliometric analyses on the emergence and present growth of humanistic management. *International Journal of Ethics and Systems, 37*(4), 581–598.

Marrucci, A., Ciappei, C., Zollo, L., & Rialti, R. (2020). Relational ontology for an ethics of work relationships. In *Philosophy and business ethics: Organizations, CSR and moral practice* (pp. 301–326). Springer International Publishing.

Marrucci, A., Rialti, R., Donvito, R., & Syed, F. U. (2022). "Connected we stand, disconnected we fall". Analyzing the importance of digital platforms in transnational supply chain management. *International Journal of Emerging Markets*. Forthcoming.

Melé, D. (2016). Understanding humanistic management. *Humanistic Management Journal, 1*, 33–55.

Nasiri, M., Ukko, J., Saunila, M., & Rantala, T. (2020). Managing the digital supply chain: The role of smart technologies. *Technovation, 96*, 102121.

Pirson, M. (2017). *Humanistic management: Protecting dignity and promoting well-being*. Cambridge University Press.

Pirson, M. A., & Lawrence, P. R. (2010). Humanism in business–towards a paradigm shift? *Journal of Business Ethics, 93*, 553–565.

Rogers, E. M. (2003). *Diffusion of innovations* (5th ed.). Free Press.

Solci, R. (2009). *I beni relazionali nella ricerca sociologica. Che cosa sono e quali effetti producono*. Tesi di Dottorato di ricerca sociologica, Università di Bologna, Dipartimento di Sociologia.

Youndt, M. A., Subramaniam, M., & Snell, S. A. (2004). Intellectual capital profiles: An examination of investments and returns. *Journal of Management Studies, 41*(2), 335–361.

Zald, M. N. (1993). Organization studies as a scientific and humanistic enterprise: Toward a reconceptualization of the foundations of the field. *Organization Science, 4*(4), 513–528.

CHAPTER 6

Perspective Management Strategies

Abstract Relational goods may influence the success of digital transformation. To do so, it is not only necessary to change the way employees relate each other, but it is also necessary for managers to implement ad hoc strategies to foster engagement and commitment in respect of change. Managers then need to change the way they are leading the company, mostly by changing the strategies they use to make knowledge flow within different areas. In the case they will be successful, and the new management style is appreciated by employees, it will be possible for them to develop an organizational environment capable to react to disruption caused by digital transformation.

Keywords Digital transformation • Organizational change • Human Resource Management • Micromanagement • Strategic change • Digital technologies • Relational goods

The results of the analyses corroborate the importance of relational goods in the current economic environment. In particular, the findings show how relational goods can initiate positive mechanisms within SMEs wishing to digitalize by introducing new technologies into their processes (Hu et al., 2023).

Qualitative analysis has shown how it is impossible to develop relational goods within a company when case managers are not involved in the

A. Marrucci, R. Rialti, *Successful Digital Transformation Initiatives in SMEs*, https://doi.org/10.1007/978-3-031-36465-5_6

nurturing of relationships between employees (Yamamoto, 2011). While relational goods may exist between two employees at any moment, in order to bring them to an organizational level, it is necessary for managers to open up to others and open up dialogue with individuals (Cordeiro, 2014). This approach is fundamental, as it facilitates the development of relational goods between managers and employees. Likewise, managers should incentivize ways for employees to socialize (King & Sethi, 1998). Socialization is the first step in the development of any human relationship and, as such, managers should encourage social interaction within the business, even during working hours, to encourage people to get in touch with other peers working in different business units (Kabadayi et al., 2019). Managers following this approach create work environments where people respect each other and communicate their opinions and knowledge in order to create new solutions (Dossena et al., 2019).

When people start to get involved in the process of creation of relational goods, and they start to recognize each other's competences, managers should set up internal reporting mechanisms, either anonymous or not. These mechanisms allow managers to identify the people who might be promoted or could become more empowered during the transformation project. What matters the most in this case is honesty from employees and justness from managers when evaluating information (Fisk et al., 2019).

This approach could allow managers to gather the necessary information on employees and organizational functions without falling into the perils of micromanagement (White Jr, 2010). Indeed, micromanagement is a management style that involves a manager closely controlling and directing the work of their employees. Micromanagement may be used to ensure that employees are on task and following instructions; thus, it may endorse person-based control in the business. One of the main problems associated with micromanagement is that it can lead to a lack of motivation and job satisfaction among employees. When employees are micromanaged, they may feel as though their work is not valued or appreciated, as they are constantly being watched and monitored. This can lead to a decrease in productivity, as employees become resentful and unmotivated (Atinc et al., 2012). They may also lose their incentive to take responsibility for their work, becoming dependent on the manager. Another problem associated with micromanagement is that it can lead to an unhealthy work environment. When employees are micromanaged, they may feel as though they have no say in their work, which can lead to frustration and resentment (White Jr, 2010). This can create an atmosphere of distrust and can impede communication, leading to a decrease in productivity. Focusing on relational goods, which provide high levels of empowerment for employees and facilitate fast communication, could mitigate these perils while ensuring the same result (Kabadayi et al., 2019).

Managers therefore play a critical role in implementing human-centered strategies and creating an environment that encourages employees and customers to succeed (Taormina, 2009). In order to develop human-centered strategies within a business, managers must take firm action. While relational goods change the way the company is working in a top-down way (i.e., new relationships between employees are the foundation of change within the organization), we can see that the initiative needs to stem from a manager in a top-down way (Allen & Meyer, 1990). Managers need to be the first agent of change and should be actively involved in this change, thus overcoming even some postulates of transformational leadership which posits that managers should somehow stay hands-off when it comes to day-to-day actions (Waddock, 2016).

Among the main duties of managers, leaders should ensure that their employees are given the resources and support they need to succeed in everyday tasks. This includes providing adequate training, providing access to tools and technology, and creating an environment where employees feel valued and respected. Managers should also foster an inclusive workplace culture that encourages everyone to contribute and offers equal opportunities for development and growth (Dierksmeier, 2020).

Secondly, managers should strive to create an environment where employees feel valued and respected. This includes providing employees with quality services and addressing their concerns in a timely manner. Furthermore, managers should seek to obtain feedback from employees regularly to help them to better understand staff needs and preferences with regard to change.

Thirdly, managers should prioritize employee engagement, providing employees with meaningful tasks aligned with opportunities for advancement. Managers should also take steps to ensure that employees have an effective work-life balance (Carr et al., 2017). They could offer flexible working hours and provide employees with access to resources and support to help them manage their work and personal lives.

Finally, managers should use fine-grained and non-biased information to make informed decisions and create strategies that are tailored to the specific needs of the business (Bachmann et al., 2018).

Managers thus have a key role to play in creating a positive work environment during times of change. By maintaining a focus on personal involvement, managers can ensure that employees are informed, supported, and understand the changes being made and their impact on the organization. In these moments, they should be transparent and open about the changes that are taking place (Selimović et al., 2021). By providing clear and accurate information about these changes, managers can ensure that employees understand the implications for the organization and for their own roles. This can help to reduce uncertainty and dispel any rumors that may be circulating (McFarland, 1977). Managers should also be available to answer any questions and address any concerns that employees may have about the changes. By listening to these concerns and addressing them, managers can help to create a sense of trust and camaraderie among the workforce. This can also help to alleviate any feelings of fear or resentment that could arise from the changes. Still, managers should involve employees in the change process. By encouraging employees to provide input and feedback, managers can ensure that employees have a sense of ownership with regard to the changes that are taking place. This can help to instill feelings of unity and purpose within the organization (Pambreni et al., 2019).

Finally, managers should recognize the impact that the changes may have on employees. By providing support and resources, managers can help to alleviate any stress that may arise from the changes. This can also help to ensure that employees feel valued and appreciated.

A manager's role in change management is therefore driving and sustaining successful change initiatives. Managers must possess the knowledge, skills, and experience required to lead the organization through times of transition and to foster an environment of trust and collaboration among employees. Managers must create a clear vision of the desired future state and ensure that their teams are aligned with the objectives of the change initiative (Vukomanovic et al., 2016). Additionally, they must be able to effectively manage resistance to the shift and handle any changes in personnel that may be necessary.

Managers wishing to build their transformation strategies on relational goods should focus on the following practice-based actions:

1. *Creating Relational Goods*: The first good practice that management needs to enact is the creation of relational goods; the successive actions will thereby follow. To do so, managers should recognize

the need to discard the notion of organization based on power hierarchies and create a model in which a collective of people can work together to achieve a common goal (Tagliagambe & Usai, 2011). It is vital to give importance to the company's relational capital by building a collaborative environment. Gui and Stanca (2010) state that "collaboration allows employees to form relationships and increases the chances of developing relational assets." Therefore, managers should view their employees as more valuable than financial resources, valuing them as a collective and for the unique qualities they bring to the community. Donati (2017, p. 28) believes that "in the society of the future, work must be drastically altered so that work activities become interconnections within a constantly changing complex system." Essentially, Donati (2017) argues that managers should move away from the traditional logic of performance-based work and prioritize a humanizing culture of work to unlock new activities and the diffusion of technological changes. This entails placing value on the human person and their creative potential.

2. *Foster Open Communication*: Encourage employees to speak openly and honestly about what they think and feel. This can be done through regular one-on-one meetings and team meetings where employees can share and work together to come up with solutions (Elshof & Hendrawan, 2022).

3. *Provide Meaningful Work*: Employees want to feel like their work has a purpose and is making a difference. Provide employees with meaningful tasks and projects that they can take ownership of (Lysova et al., 2019).

4. *Recognize and Reward Excellence*: When employees do something well, recognize them publicly and reward them with something that is meaningful to them. This could be a gift card, a day off, or even a simple thank you (Gupta & Bose, 2022).

5. *Offer Flexible Working Hours*: Giving employees the freedom to work when and where they want can be a great way to increase engagement. A flexible work schedule can help employees balance their personal and work lives and feel more fulfilled (Papagiannidis et al., 2020).

6. *Create a Positive Work Environment*: A positive work environment is essential for keeping employees engaged. Managers should take steps to ensure employees feel supported, respected, and listened to (Winasis et al., 2020).

7. *Encourage Professional Development*: Investing in your employees' professional development is a great way to show them you care about their growth and development. Offer employees training and education opportunities or allow them to attend conferences and workshops related to their field (Baiyere et al., 2020).
8. *Promote Teamwork*: Encourage employees to collaborate and work together to achieve goals. Team-building activities and events can help foster a strong team dynamic and increase engagement (Hadjielias et al., 2021).
9. *Show Appreciation*: Showing appreciation for employees' hard work and dedication is a great way to increase engagement. Regularly thank your employees for their hard work and let them know how much you value their contributions (Berman, 2012).

Building humanism and relational goods-centered environments is neither easy nor immediate. Managers need to sense the need for change in the way relationships are run, change their approach to management, and alter the ways employees relate to each other and to managers (Kabadayi et al., 2019). In this way, communication and trust will be improved.

These strategies support organizational change, as people feel committed to the organization and will therefore be ready to put in effort toward shared goals.

This phenomenon derives from a new sense-making approach to individual work. Sense-making emerges when everyone in a company (including top management) is perceived to be pushing in the same direction in order to create something new and meaningful. Change may occur, and the business may adapt and become ready to face new challenges emerging in its environment, such as the quest for digitalization. Answering the first research question, humanistic principles can be applied in SMEs. These have a beneficial effect when suitably applied by managers.

The business world before the COVID-19 pandemic was focused only on profit and on actions taken to increase profitability. The perception of an overreaching danger and of common problems generated a new sense of community, which required businesses to adapt in order to continue to attract talent. In this regard, while a humanism-centered approach might not solve all of a firm's problems, this approach can at least provide a way for interested businesses to overtly pay attention to emerging employee requests, helping firms to set themselves apart from competitors. The selection of humanist and relational goods-centered approaches, with respect to the adoption of new technologies, could allow employees to overcome resistance and criticism surrounding these tools by helping them to understand the need behind the transformation. Similarly, the increased focus of managers with respect to employees fosters the development of different feelings pertaining to transformation. Employees working in human-centered organizations will not perceive technology to be a substitute for their skills, but rather a support that could make their work easier.

That is, having human-technology collaboration prevents alienation, and one of the few possible ways to foster such an approach is represented by investments in humans and helping them to make their competences more important than artificial agents (Rapp, 1985).

While these actions can be performed either by large businesses or SMEs, for the latter, they can mean the difference between survival and disappearance. This is because SME managers are more prone to implement micromanagement strategies, which does improve managerial control but mostly creates negative environments (McFarland, 1977). SMEs are characterized by greater levels of resistance to change than larger counterparts. Indeed, these businesses are frequently populated by older workforces that are extremely resistant when it is time to change the way that they have always worked. Finally, these businesses frequently fail to attract, and then maintain, new employees (as they are often attracted by job-offers from larger companies). Building a relational goods-orientated climate could thus allow firms to reduce turnaround intention and nurture a team for the future. Henceforth, the second research question has been answered, as relational goods could allow SME managers to address many of the problems arising during phases of digital transformation (Elshof & Hendrawan, 2022).

REFERENCES

Allen, N. J., & Meyer, J. P. (1990). Organizational socialization tactics: A longitudinal analysis of links to newcomers' commitment and role orientation. *Academy of Management Journal, 33*(4), 847–858.

Atinc, G., Simmering, M. J., & Kroll, M. J. (2012). Control variable use and reporting in macro and micro management research. *Organizational Research Methods, 15*(1), 57–74.

Bachmann, C., Sasse, L., & Habisch, A. (2018). Applying the practical wisdom lenses in decision-making: An integrative approach to humanistic management. *Humanistic Management Journal, 2*, 125–150.

Baiyere, A., Salmela, H., & Tapanainen, T. (2020). Digital transformation and the new logics of business process management. *European Journal of Information Systems, 29*(3), 238–259.

Berman, S. J. (2012). Digital transformation: Opportunities to create new business models. *Strategy & Leadership, 40*(2), 16–24.

Carr, S. C., Parker, J., Arrowsmith, J., Haar, J., & Jones, H. (2017). Humanistic management and living wages: A case of compelling connections? *Humanistic Management Journal, 1*, 215–236.

Cordeiro, J. (2014). The boundaries of the human: From humanism to transhumanism. *World Future Review, 6*(3), 231–239.

Dierksmeier, C. (2020). From Jensen to Jensen: Mechanistic management education or humanistic management learning? *Journal of Business Ethics, 166*(1), 73–87.

Donati, P. (2017). *Quale lavoro? L'emergere di una economia relazionale.* Marietti.

Dossena, C., Mizzau, L., & Mochi, F. (2019). Social media in HRM: A humanistic management perspective. In *HRM 4.0 for human-centered organizations* (Vol. 23, pp. 201–219). Emerald Publishing Limited.

Elshof, M., & Hendrawan, B. (2022). Humanistic communication professionals: Dialogue and listening skills as core competencies of humanistic communication professionals in the Netherlands. *Journal of Communication Management, 26*, 236–253.

Fisk, R., Fuessel, A., Laszlo, C., Struebi, P., Valera, A., & Weiss, C. (2019). Systemic social innovation: Co-creating a future where humans and all life thrive. *Humanistic Management Journal, 4*, 191–214.

Gui, B., & Stanca, L. (2010). Happiness and relational goods: Well-being and interpersonal relations in the economic sphere. *International Review of Economics, 57*, 105–118.

Gupta, G., & Bose, I. (2022). Digital transformation in entrepreneurial firms through information exchange with operating environment. *Information & Management, 59*(3), 103243.

Hadjielias, E., Dada, O. L., Cruz, A. D., Zekas, S., Christofi, M., & Sakka, G. (2021). How do digital innovation teams function? Understanding the team cognition-process nexus within the context of digital transformation. *Journal of Business Research, 122*, 373–386.

Hu, L., Olivieri, M., & Rialti, R. (2023). Dynamically adapting to the new normal: Unpacking SMEs' adoption of social media during COVID-19 outbreaks. *Journal of Business & Industrial Marketing.* Forthcoming.

Kabadayi, S., Alkire, L., Broad, G. M., Livne-Tarandach, R., Wasieleski, D., & Puente, A. M. (2019). Humanistic management of social innovation in service

(SIS): An interdisciplinary framework. *Humanistic Management Journal,* *4*, 159–185.

King, R. C., & Sethi, V. (1998). The impact of socialization on the role adjustment of information systems professionals. *Journal of Management Information Systems, 14*(4), 195–217.

Lysova, E. I., Allan, B. A., Dik, B. J., Duffy, R. D., & Steger, M. F. (2019). Fostering meaningful work in organizations: A multi-level review and integration. *Journal of Vocational Behavior, 110,* 374–389.

McFarland, D. E. (1977). Management, humanism, and society: The case for macromanagement theory. *Academy of Management Review, 2*(4), 613–623.

Pambreni, Y., Khatibi, A., Azam, S., & Tham, J. J. M. S. L. (2019). The influence of total quality management toward organization performance. *Management Science Letters, 9*(9), 1397–1406.

Papagiannidis, S., Harris, J., & Morton, D. (2020). WHO led the digital transformation of your company? A reflection of IT related challenges during the pandemic. *International Journal of Information Management, 55,* 102166.

Rapp, F. (1985). Humanism and technology: The two-cultures debate. *Technology in Society, 7*(4), 423–435.

Selimović, J., Pilav-Velić, A., & Krndžija, L. (2021). Digital workplace transformation in the financial service sector: Investigating the relationship between employees' expectations and intentions. *Technology in Society, 66,* 101640.

Tagliagambe, S., & Usai, G. (2011). Soggetti umani e soggetti collettivi nell'impresa e oltre l'impresa. *Sinergie Italian Journal of Management, 79,* 173–191.

Taormina, R. J. (2009). Organizational socialization: The missing link between employee needs and organizational culture. *Journal of Managerial Psychology, 24*(7), 650–676.

Vukomanovic, M., Young, M., & Huynink, S. (2016). IPMA ICB 4.0—A global standard for project, programme and portfolio management competences. *International Journal of Project Management, 34*(8), 1703–1705.

Waddock, S. (2016). Developing humanistic leadership education. *Humanistic Management Journal, 1,* 57–73.

White, R. D., Jr. (2010). The micromanagement disease: Symptoms, diagnosis, and cure. *Public Personnel Management, 39*(1), 71–76.

Winasis, S., Riyanto, S., & Ariyanto, E. (2020). Digital transformation in the Indonesian banking industry: Impact on employee engagement. *International Journal of Innovation, Creativity and Change, 12*(4), 528–543.

Yamamoto, H. (2011). The relationship between employee benefit management and employee retention. *The International Journal of Human Resource Management, 22*(17), 3550–3564.

CHAPTER 7

Conclusions

Abstract Relational goods may play a role in digital transformation processes of SMEs. In particular, managers should invest in nurturing relationships between themselves and employees, and among employees. Whether these initiatives will be successful, it will be possible to create an environment in which it may be possible to engage all the subjects in digital transformation.

Keywords Digital transformation • Change management • Organizational climate • Relational goods • Business ethics • SMEs

The purpose of this book was to explore the importance of relational goods in SMEs facing digital transformation processes. The results observed that relational goods can trigger several micro-mechanisms within a business. These mechanisms are capable of fostering the success of these endeavors.

Relational goods can influence the entire climate of the work environment. The presence of such immaterial goods, by affecting the ways people relate to each other at work and by weighing interpersonal relationships, can generate information-sharing behavior and, in turn, a greater commitment to change. Indeed, the development of organizational mechanisms to share knowledge is fundamental to ensuring that everyone can access

A. Marrucci, R. Rialti, *Successful Digital Transformation Initiatives in SMEs*, https://doi.org/10.1007/978-3-031-36465-5_7

83

the information required to develop a favorable mindset with regard to change.

The importance of managers' actions with respect to the development of relational goods has also been observed. Managers cannot be detached from their employees when trying to achieve this kind of transformation. Otherwise, employees will not trust them, and the development of relational goods between the first and the second may not occur (Frederico, 2021).

We observed how relational goods may be an alternative approach to traditional management practices. Indeed, these goods may represent the cornerstone, differentiating between businesses wishing to transform and those not capable of doing so.

The book therefore contributes to the nascent stream of literature on humanist management in technology strategy. It differentiates from previous research by being empirical and providing implications from real-world cases. Additionally, it makes a contribution by identifying which humanistic approach should be used when it comes to the digital transformation of SMEs.

In light of future avenues of research, we can consider how scholars and practitioners can focus on diverse humanistic-bound actions that can be undertaken in the business. Similarly, we can also explore whether the importance of relational goods is greater or lesser in different contexts. Employees' different cultural backgrounds may, in fact, affect the ways in which people interact with each other, with differing degrees of importance attributed to these goods. Scholars may also consider different theories and methods that could be used to evaluate the importance of relational goods. While the Diffusion of Innovation Theory is a parsimonious model to consider, the factors underlying digital transformation and the examination of these factors through other approaches could bring about different results.

Reference

Frederico, G. F. (2021). Project Management for Supply Chains 4.0: A conceptual framework proposal based on PMBOK methodology. *Operations Management Research, 14*(3–4), 434–450.

INDEX

GPSR Compliance
The European Union's (EU) General Product Safety Regulation (GPSR) is a set
of rules that requires consumer products to be safe and our obligations to
ensure this.

If you have any concerns about our products, you can contact us on

ProductSafety@springernature.com

In case Publisher is established outside the EU, the EU authorized
representative is:

Springer Nature Customer Service Center GmbH
Europaplatz 3
69115 Heidelberg, Germany